TO:

_____

FROM:

_____

GOD'S DREAM
FOR YOU

FINDING
LASTING
CHANGE IN
JESUS

MATTHEW BARNETT

A Division of Thomas Nelson Publishers
Since 1798

www.thomasnelson.com

THOMAS NELSON
Since 1798

Published in Nashville, Tennessee, by Thomas Nelson. Thomas Nelson is a registered trademark of Thomas Nelson, Inc.

Cover design by Mary Hooper, Milkglass Creative.

Thomas Nelson, Inc., titles may be purchased in bulk for educational, business, fund-raising, or sales promotional use. For information, please e-mail SpecialMarkets@ ThomasNelson.com.

Unless otherwise noted, Scripture quotations are taken from the NEW KING JAMES VERSION. © 1982 by Thomas Nelson, Inc. Used by permission. All rights reserved.

Scripture quotations marked NLT are taken from the *Holy Bible*, New Living Translation, copyright © 1996, 2004, 2007 by Tyndale House Foundation. Used by permission of Tyndale House Publishers, Inc., Carol Stream, Illinois 60188. All rights reserved.

Scripture quotations marked TLB are taken from *The Living Bible* ©1971. Used by permission of Tyndale House Publishers, Wheaton, IL. All rights reserved.

Scripture quotations marked NIV are taken from the Holy Bible, New International Version®. Copyright © 1973, 1978, 1984, 2011 by Biblica, Inc.™ Used by permission of Zondervan. All rights reserved worldwide. www.zondervan.com

Scripture quotations marked PHILLIPS are taken from J. B. Phillips: THE NEW TESTAMENT IN MODERN ENGLISH, Revised Edition © J. B. Phillips 1958, 1960, 1972. Used by permission of Macmillan Publishing Co., Inc.

Scripture quotations marked MSG are taken from *The Message* by Eugene H. Peterson. © 1993, 1994, 1995, 1996, 2000. Used by permission of NavPress Publishing Group. All rights reserved.

ISBN-13: 978-1-4003-2080-6

Printed in China

13 14 15 16 RRD 5 4 3 2 1

www.thomasnelson.com

Table of Contents

"What Am I Doing Here?"

IF YOU KNEW FOR SURE THAT GOD HIMSELF HAD a dream for your life that predated the birth of the stars, galaxies, and planets, wouldn't it be worth finding out what it might be?

I certainly never thought I would find God's dream for me while I was standing on a stained, littered sidewalk on Skid Row in Los Angeles. But there I stood. And as I watched my dad drive away, I felt more alone and desolate than I had ever felt in my twenty years.

What in the world is a sheltered suburban kid like me doing here—by myself—in the mean streets of central Los Angeles? And whose vision of ministry was I following anyway—my own or my dad's?

In reality, the vision belonged to both of us.

When Dad was a twenty-year-old evangelist—no older than I was when I stood on that Skid Row sidewalk—he had driven through the streets of Los Angeles, passing by the historic Angelus Temple and Echo Park. God whispered to my dad's heart that someday he would pastor a church in that part of LA.

Now, forty years later, that vision was about to be fulfilled. Only the pastor wasn't Tommy Barnett. It was me, Matthew Barnett, his son. *If* I could stick it out . . . which was very much an open question at that moment.

I'd wanted to be a pastor since I was sixteen, and I'd hung around the church with my dad for as long as I could remember. Dad had about fourteen thousand people in the congregation at that time—a megachurch by anyone's standards. Little Bethel Temple was to be my first pastorate even though I had never pastored a day in my life. The fact is, I would do just about anything for my dad, and I had promised him I would try this for three months—*just* three months—while he looked for someone more qualified.

But this three-month stint really wasn't his idea alone. I too had experienced a vision for Los Angeles.

Four years earlier, on a hot summer night in Phoenix, I was lying on the hood of my car under the stars, thinking about my future. In those moments God gave me a vision of a city in need, and strangely, it wasn't my own hometown. It was Los Angeles. Up until that time, I'd always associated LA with Disneyland, Universal Studios, Beverly Hills, and the Pacific Ocean. I'd never thought about the inner city, let alone ministering to gangs, prostitutes, and people in housing projects, so I knew that this whole train of thought had to be from the Lord.

The vision showed me that someday I would be in Los Angeles, pastoring a church in the heart of the city.

That's another reason I agreed to step into the job at Bethel Temple until that more experienced, better qualified pastor came along, stepped into the pulpit, and allowed me to return home to Phoenix.

Trouble was, no one wanted the job.

Who would want to lead an impoverished church in the middle of this depressed, crime-ridden neighborhood in central LA near Skid Row?

Just moments before he drove away, Dad placed his hands on my shoulders, and we prayed together right there on the sidewalk, with the buzz and clatter of the city all around us. After he said, "Amen," he pulled his car keys out of his pocket and jingled them in his right hand, hesitating.

"Are you okay, Son?"

I had a lump in my throat the size of a golf ball, but I nodded, smiled, and said, "I'm good."

"You sure?"

"I'm sure."

He got into the car, gave me an encouraging little smile and wave, and drove off down Bellevue Avenue. I stared after him, watching his car fade into the traffic.

At least I *thought* he drove off. What he actually did (and I didn't learn this until years later) was drive a couple blocks down the road, pull over to the curb, turn off the ignition, put his face in his hands, and begin sobbing. He told me later that he cried so hard he thought he was having a nervous breakdown.

"Oh, God," he prayed. "*What have I done?* I've set him

up for failure. I've scarred him for the rest of his life. This is going to hurt him—badly—because he can't make it in this neighborhood. He can't relate to the people in this community! He's the only white guy for ten miles in any direction! He's never been in this kind of environment before! Oh, Lord, what have I done to my boy?"

Inner city Los Angeles was indeed a desperate, dangerous place, and I was more than a little naive, woefully inexperienced, and barely out of my teens. Dad said that leaving me there on the sidewalk by myself was about a hundred times worse than dropping a child off at kindergarten for the first time.

After all, Bethel Temple was located in a high crime area, surrounded by liquor stores, and with a heavy gang presence for miles around. Birthed in the glory days of the Azusa Street Revival in the early 1900s, the church was only a shell of its former prominence. When I stepped into the pastorate, about twenty people showed up . . . on a good Sunday. After they got a look at their new pastor, even those twenty stalwarts began to melt away.

When I stepped into the pastorate, about twenty people showed up . . . on a good Sunday.

Dad might have changed his mind about the whole crazy idea, driven around the block, picked me up, and taken me back to Phoenix with him if the Lord hadn't spoken to his heart in that exact moment. He told Dad, "Tommy, give him his chance. You never know what's inside a person. You never know what a person can accomplish."

So, driving out Interstate 10 toward Phoenix, Dad did his best to give his doubts and fears to the Lord. By the time he got to Palm Desert, he began to relax his death grip on the steering wheel. *Something great could happen in that place even if I don't see it now, even if I don't feel it now. Maybe there's something more going on here than I realize.*

Later that day, which had actually been my first day on the job, I was in the church's little office trying to get organized. Suddenly several loud pops sent me running for the church's front door. People who have never been around gunfire always say the shots sound like firecrackers, and they're right. Throwing the door open, I was just in time to see a young teenage boy murdered outside the church doors. The acrid smell of gunpowder still hung in the air.

I remember crying out to God, "Lord, *what am I doing here?* What am I doing in this place? How can I ever hope to make a difference here?"

One night a few days later, I found myself suddenly wide awake in the middle of the night. I felt like God was speaking to me, telling me to walk to Echo Park, over near Dodger Stadium. It certainly wasn't a safe thing to do. At that time Echo Park was populated by gangs, prostitutes, and the many homeless people who had nowhere else to go. But I knew that since God was calling me, He would also protect me.

Out in the darkness of that place with the sound of the city all around me, the city that never sleeps, the Lord spoke to me. I seemed to hear Him say, "Matthew, I didn't bring you to the inner city to build a great church, but to build people. These people. You build the people; I will build the church. I don't ever want you to think about success again. Think about being a blessing. Success is obedience to your calling. I've called you to bless people. Love them. Heal them. Help them. Serve them."

It was a tall order for this unlikely and very green young man who had just entered a strange new world, but I went back to bed that night with a new flame of encouragement flickering in my heart. The Lord Himself had brought me here. Hadn't I just heard Him say so? And He hadn't brought me to this place to be a famous pastor or walk in my dad's huge footsteps, but simply to be a blessing to some hurting, desperate people.

With His help, I knew I could do that much.

———

God had a dream for my life, a dream that was so much wider, higher, and deeper than I had ever imagined. And I still can't imagine where it's going, because I'm up to my ears in it even as I write these words.

Please believe me when I say the same is true for you: God has a dream for you this very moment.

When King David came to that realization, he found himself filled with wonder:

He hadn't brought
me to this place to
be a famous pastor
or walk in my dad's
huge footsteps,
but simply to
be a blessing to
some hurting,
desperate people.

You saw me before I was born.
Every day of my life was recorded in your book.
Every moment was laid out
before a single day had passed.
How precious are your thoughts about me, O God.
They cannot be numbered!
I can't even count them.

PSALM 139:16–18 NLT

So, back to my initial question.

If you knew for sure that God Himself had a dream for your life that predated the birth of the stars, galaxies, and planets, wouldn't it be worth finding out what that dream might be?

You can find out by starting at the simplest level of all: Just ask God. Ask Him to tell you what His dream for your life is. Cry out to Him.

Who knows where it will take you.

Wherever it does, you can be sure it will be the place where you truly belong.

What Is Your Dream?

I T'S THE ONE QUESTION THEY NEVER EXPECT.

You can see their eyes widen when we ask them. They suddenly look up as if to say, "Did I hear you right? Did you really just ask me what I thought you asked me?"

Most of the time, when a homeless family arrives on our Los Angeles campus, they've lost just about everything. They have their car, whatever they've been able to cram into it, and nothing much else except the clothes on their backs.

Someone on our staff takes them into a room and sits down with them. They're expecting all of the usual questions they'd get from most social workers. *Here we go again. Another person with another pen and another clipboard. I know the drill: "Name? Marital status? Children? Ages of children? Previous address? Previous employer? Previous occupation? Health status?" Etc., etc.*

But we don't do that kind of intake here. We have a different first question, and it almost always takes people by surprise.

"What is your dream?"

The question stuns them. Confuses them. Then often their eyes narrow a little with a flash of suspicion. *Is this a joke? Is this sarcasm? Is this person mocking me when I'm down?*

What is my dream? Are you kidding me? Coming here isn't about dreaming! It's about surviving. It's about staying alive and keeping body and soul together. I didn't show up on the front porch of a place like this because I'm chasing my dream. I've ended up here because I don't have anywhere else to go. I want to keep my family together. I want to keep my marriage together. I want my hungry kids to be fed. I want to get off the streets! I don't want to end up in prison like some people I know. I don't want to live with abuse or threats. And I don't have the energy any longer to fight the alcoholism, drug abuse, and the prostitution that are all around me.

And you ask me, "What is your dream?" Why do you even ask me that when I'm just trying to survive?

But "What is your dream?" is no idle question. It pertains to life and death. In Proverbs 29:18 we read: "Where there is no revelation [or vision], the people cast off restraint."

In other words, without a dream, people don't exercise self-control. When men and women have nothing to live for, they "cast off restraint."

So right up front we ask the people who come to us, "What is your dream? What do you want to see happen in your life? What do you want to achieve? Where do you want to go?"

"Well," they may say, "we're just trying to survive."

And we answer: "But what if we took survival off the table? While you're here, you won't have to worry about that. This is a safe, clean place, and we will give you the food and shelter you need. So let's start thinking about your potential."

The fact is, when you've been disappointed again and again, you become afraid to dream. After all, how could you bear another disappointment? But in the power of Christ, you can begin to dream again.

Even in marriages, there comes a point where people lose hope. A husband and wife may be committed to staying together for the rest of their lives, but as they imagine the years ahead, it looks to them more like running an endurance test or slogging along on an endless marathon under gray, rainy skies. Life looks more like grim survival than anything else. The idea that they could ever thrive in their marriage seems so far out there that it doesn't even seem real.

Asking people "What is your dream?" is almost like lifting them to a whole different plane. We've found that most people really do have something in their heart they would love to do or pursue, but they have suppressed that dream for so long that it doesn't seem like a possibility at all. Maybe the dream is getting free of addiction. Maybe it's finishing high school or going to college. Maybe it's being trained for a certain occupation or specific career. The desire is still there, but it's buried so deeply beneath

Without a dream, people don't exercise self-control. When men and women have nothing to live for, they "cast off restraint."

their setbacks, pain, and loss that they've forgotten they ever had any aspirations.

But once we hear their dream, we tell them, "We're going to help you get to your dream"—and they can hardly believe their ears. Maybe they expected to have to prove themselves first or completely clean up their life before we would start talking to them about their future.

This "What is your dream?" interaction is based on a concept that the Lord has impressed on us through the years as we've worked with people in crisis. We call it "belong and believe." In the Gospels, Jesus said to a number of men, "Come and follow Me," and at that point these men were in no way ready to be disciples of Christ. They were just regular guys. Some of them fished for a living. Matthew had been a tax collector for the Romans, a traitor hated and resented by virtually everyone. But Jesus called each one of them, inviting them to be close to Him, to walk with Him, to get to know Him better, and to serve Him.

That's what Jesus did, but that's not what religion

usually does. Instead religion will say, "When you believe what we believe, then we'll let you belong and be involved in what we're doing." But Jesus allowed people to belong first, to see what He was doing, find themselves drawn to Him, and then believe.

I love how the apostle John captured this order of events in his gospel:

> The next day John [the Baptist] was there again with two of his disciples. When he saw Jesus passing by, he said, "Look, the Lamb of God!"
>
> When the two disciples heard him say this, they followed Jesus. Turning around, Jesus saw them following and asked, "What do you want?"
>
> They said, "Rabbi" (which means "Teacher"), "where are you staying?"
>
> "Come," he replied, "and you will see."
>
> So they went and saw where he was staying, and they spent that day with him. It was about four in the afternoon. (John 1:35–39 NIV)

That is so like the Lord. He says, "Come, and you will see." In the Psalms He says, "Taste and see that the LORD

is good. Oh, the joys of those who take refuge in him!"
(Psalm 34:8 NLT).

Jesus allowed people to belong first, before they
believed. Then, as they walked with Him, they began to
believe. For some of them, coming to faith in Jesus took
a long time. Two disciples didn't believe until after the
resurrection when Jesus directly confronted them and
said, "How foolish you are, and how slow to believe all
that the prophets have spoken!" (Luke 24:25 NIV). He
didn't justify their lack of belief or make excuses for their
behavior while they were learning, but He allowed them
to belong in order to believe. They didn't have to clean
up their lives first.

And then, maybe sooner, maybe later, as men and
women see Christ and His followers up close, they realize
that God Himself has a dream for their lives. Belonging
encourages believing.

Manuel Ramos was seventeen when he came into our
teen discipleship program. (This is a major program at

the Dream Center where teens who have been kicked out of their home and kicked out of school are raised in a Christian environment.) Manny's father was an alcoholic, and as a young boy, Manny himself became heavily involved in alcohol and drug abuse. He has been hospitalized more times than he can remember, he once accidentally burned down his home, and he drifted from trailer park to trailer park staying with friends until he ended up on the mean streets. He was probably as lost and broken and lonely as a young man can be.

When Manny finally came to us—thanks to the help of a concerned family friend—dreams were the last thing on his mind. All too real was the horrific nightmare from which he had just emerged.

"I had no idea I even had a dream," he says. "I shouldn't even be alive! At one point in my life, I was so messed up I thought it was all over. I couldn't remember what I had done that week because I had never been sober. I was homeless, no one cared about me, and I didn't care about myself. I didn't take care of my body or try to stay clean. I just didn't care."

And Manny had become an alcoholic by age thirteen.

"Addiction doesn't really say it," he recalls. "It was more like *affliction*. Something awful. I was so lost—but nobody cared. If I had been dying, no one would have heard my screams. So dreams? I never had time to think about dreams. I'm only seventeen years old, but I've gone through stuff in my life that no man should ever go through. I've felt pain that's so painful you want to throw up, but I had to go on. So I quit sobbing and wiped my eyes. I hid the pain in the corner of my heart where no light shines. That's where it stayed, and I forgot it was even there."

Once in our program, though, Manny learned that he had to reencounter all of that hidden pain before he could catch a vision for a new life.

Jesus helped him do exactly that.

———

Soon after Manny met Jesus, the Lord walked him over to that corner of his heart where he had buried all his sorrow—the still-raw, jumbled up, jagged-edged, poison-tipped blades of pain that had torn into his young soul again and again.

That hiding place in Manny's heart reminds me of an article I read about storing nuclear waste out in the deserts of eastern Washington State. In a process known as vitrification, radioactive liquids and sludge are turned into large glass logs that are stored in vast vaults somewhere deep under the soil—where they will presumably remain for the next thousand years or so.

But Jesus doesn't allow hidden vaults of crystalized pain and deep-rooted anguish. He wants to throw those vaults open. He wants to take that pain on Himself.

"Jesus showed me my despair," Manny says. "I found out right then that I had a Father and that He was a Father who actually cared about me. Without Him, I would have no dreams at all. I guess I had been just too proud to let God take care of me."

Sometime in the midst of Manny's discipleship program, somebody taught him Jesus' words in Matthew 6:33–34 (NIV):

"But seek first his kingdom and his righteousness, and all these things will be given to you as well. Therefore do not worry about tomorrow, for tomorrow will worry about itself. Each day has enough trouble of its own."

As Manny began to do exactly that—to seek God first, to release all of his stored-up pain—he found something he hadn't even been looking for. Manny found his dreams.

Pain is like the bully in the room that chases a person's hopes out the door and sends dreams into hiding.

That's why people in crisis who come through our doors are so surprised to have us ask them, "What is your dream?" Their dreams have been overshadowed by their disappointments and sorrows for so long that they may have forgotten they ever had any.

But the Lord doesn't forget anything. As you ask God to reveal His dream for your life, He may first have to roll up His sleeves and help you work through some interwoven layers of heartbreak that have hidden His desire and purpose for your life.

Jesus did exactly that for Manny, even after all that young man had been through, and Jesus can do it for you.

"Why Shouldn't I Just Quit?"

There's a little Dairy Queen somewhere east of LA on the 10 freeway.

The 10 is the big east-west artery between inner city Los Angeles, where I had been breaking my heart trying to birth a ministry, and my home in Phoenix, Arizona. It's a no-nonsense, mostly straight shot through the desert that takes six to seven hours, give or take, to drive. The road passes through Banning, Palm Springs, Indio, and Blythe. The scenery? Some windmills. Some desert brush. A few mountains. Not much else.

But off some forgettable exit about an hour east of LA, there's that Dairy Queen.

One night early on in that first year of ministry,

I felt my time was up mentally. I was already past my three-month contract to help my dad, and I had checked out. I locked up my office, threw everything in my car, tried to swallow the big lump in my throat, and started driving. I knew the drill: Hollywood Freeway east, 110 south, and then merge onto Interstate 10, into the setting sun. That was the road that would take me home, away from my failure, away from all the inner city brokenness and insanity.

Dad? Yeah, he'd be disappointed, but knowing him, he'd probably blame himself. He'd maybe let me join the church staff. I could help with the youth or some outreach program. Something would work out. Somehow.

When I got to the Dairy Queen, I pulled off the road. I could use the bathroom. Maybe get a cheeseburger. But I knew there was something I needed to take care of first before I went any farther.

Sitting in my car, in that Dairy Queen parking lot at twilight, I tried to explain it to the Lord. I knew I had failed Him, failed my dad, failed the desperately needy people in LA's inner city, and failed myself. God had given me a vision, and I was dropping it like a hot potato.

I knew I was going home defeated and discouraged, giving up on what surely seemed to me like a lost cause. A real church could have been built without this inexperienced kid. But I still needed to talk to God about it.

"Okay, Lord," I finally said. "What am I going to do?"

And He said, "Just give Me one more day."

"Lord, there's no way I can pastor this church. And I can't picture anything changing in the future."

"I'm not asking you to do anything in the future. I'm just asking you for one more day."

Neither of us said anything for a while. And then I said, "Okay, just one more day. That's all I can promise You."

"And that's all I ask."

I got my cheeseburger and a Blizzard and drove back to LA.

In the days to come, I made several more such trips, car loaded, tears in my eyes, heading for Phoenix. But each time I pulled off at the Dairy Queen to explain to Jesus why I was leaving LA.

And each time He asked me for just one more day.

Why was I so discouraged?

I was twenty years old, this was my first church, and we only had eighteen people. Actually, we *started* with eighteen people. After I'd been pastoring for a few weeks, we were down to two—and they didn't look too steady.

The kicker came on a Sunday night when I sat looking out the window of that little church, waiting to see some headlights as cars pulled into the parking lot. And none came.

At 6:50, ten minutes before the seven o'clock service, still no one had arrived. No cars. No headlights. No people. At seven, I turned off all the lights. Instead of going home, however, I went out and just started knocking on doors in the community, talking about Jesus to anyone who would listen.

Later, as I looked at that darkened church, I felt like the biggest failure in the world. I had grown up in a megachurch of fourteen thousand people, where my dad had been successful for years and years.

And I had no one even show up for a service. *No one!*

That was the first time I packed my car and headed east on Interstate 10, and that was the first time the Lord met me at the Dairy Queen. I knew I'd hit bottom in my ministry, but if the Lord wanted me to give it another twenty-four hours, I could at least do that much.

Now here I am, in the same place after eighteen years. And I'm so glad—so very grateful to the Lord—that I didn't quit when I could have quit and when I desperately wanted to quit.

———

I have definitely seen the value of giving the Lord twenty-four hours either to change your circumstances or give you strength when you're feeling weak. In fact, at certain times and in the face of certain battles, all you can say is, "God, I can't give You a month, and I can't give You a week. But I can give You the next twenty-four hours."

The simple fact is, we have no idea what God's provision for us will be tomorrow morning. Scripture says that His mercies are new every morning and that His faithfulness is great (Lamentations 3:23). Who knows what those mercies will be? They might come in a trickle—or they might pour in like a flood.

Remember the prophet Elijah? He ran like a jackrabbit from his enemies and then collapsed exhausted under a desert broom tree. He made this getaway after expending great effort in what now seemed to him like a losing cause. That's when the prophet mailed in his letter of resignation: "I've had enough," he told the Lord. "Take away my life. I've got to die sometime, and it might as well be now" (1 Kings 19:4 TLB).

After Elijah napped a bit, however, an angel woke up the discouraged prophet, fed him a hot meal, and let him sleep some more. Then the angel woke him up again, gave him another meal, and said, "Okay, time to get back on the road." And, in the strength of that heavenly meal, Elijah went on a long, long way.

The Lord didn't accept Elijah's letter of resignation; there was still work to be done, and there was still life to be lived. What I take from the story is this: just because you run out of strength and hope and the will to go on today doesn't mean the Lord won't give you all you need tomorrow.

One of the things we ask our people in rehab to do is to give their testimonies on stage in front of all the others. Sometimes they may only be three or four weeks into the program. Some people have criticized us for that, saying, "You should wait until they're *proven* followers before they give their testimonies. You should wait until they have a track record."

But here's how we see it: somebody who has been in the rehab program for three or four weeks is *already* a work of grace. Their stories encourage everyone, and I can't tell you how many people in our program have changed their minds about giving up or quitting after hearing one of their fellow students talk about staying clean and sober, about how the Lord has worked in their lives.

But the listeners aren't the only ones who benefit.

Sometimes the people I ask to share have been a hair's breadth away from quitting themselves. But when they get up and talk about what the Lord has been doing in their lives during the preceding few weeks, they're reminded of how far they have already come. And when they hear everybody clapping and cheering for them, shouting words of encouragement or wiping away tears of joy, they say to themselves, *What was I thinking of? I can't quit now!*

I could share many stories of people I've met through the years who, like Elijah, were ready to give up and resign from life, who in fact wished for death. I think of Joyce Dunigan, a forty-one-year-old woman who works with our food truck ministry.

Her dad abandoned the family when Joyce was only nine years old, and it was the worst moment of her young life. She adored her daddy, but he walked away from Joyce, her little sister Sylvia, and her mother—and he never looked back.

As if that weren't trauma enough, throughout their entire childhood, Joyce and her sister were sexually abused by their grandfather—and the abuse got much worse after their dad walked away. To cope with the pain, Joyce began smoking cigarettes and weed and drinking at age twelve. By the time she was sixteen, she was shooting up heroin and cocaine. Being half Irish, half Hispanic, and raised by a Hispanic mom, Joyce found it easy to fit in with the Mexican gangs in her hometown of Norwalk.

"I chose to hang out with friends whose family members were gang bangers," she recalls. "Embracing the gang culture, I always played the role that I was hard. That nothing bothered me. That nothing could hurt me. I proved myself in the gang culture by committing crimes ranging from drive-bys to robberies. There were so many, many times when I stared death in the face. I thought it was funny and had no concept at all that God was protecting me through those days.

"I was in and out of jail, in and out of rehabs. My addictions became so bad that no one wanted to help me anymore. After getting kicked out of my last-chance rehab option, I had nowhere left to go. Like so many others, I ended up on Skid Row, and I lived there for seven months. Sometimes I just wanted to die, but somehow I stayed alive.

"Then, when my condition became desperate, I remembered something a lady in my family's church said to me about a Dream Center on Bellevue, off the Hollywood Freeway, and I ended up on the doorstep there, and they took me in. Even though everyone was so kind to me, I still acted my part—that I was hard as nails and didn't care about anyone or anything.

"Going through the rehab program was the hardest thing I have ever done. I made a lot of mistakes, I had a lot of setbacks, but I graduated."

And during that time Joyce's heart was changing in amazing ways.

"It seemed crazy to me that people here loved me and were rooting for me to change. And I did change, but it wasn't from the outside in, the way I thought it would be. I changed from the inside out.

"I now had Jesus in my life, and my *thinking* started to change. I started believing what God says about me, about who I really am in Christ. And then I started wanting to act and look different. My attitude toward people changed. I loved and respected people. Where had the hate gone? I graduated both years of the discipleship program, and then I got my GED, graduating on stage before hundreds of cheering, excited brothers and sisters. Just recently, I started a college program! Looking back, the best thing I remember about that whole experience was that people didn't try to change me; the presence of the Lord did that.

"Pastor Matthew gave me the chance to become a part of the food truck ministry. And now . . . *now* I understand why God let me go through all that I've gone through in my life. I really relate to the people I serve at my sites. I know that some of them are ready to quit, just like I was. Reaching out to them and helping them has made me a better, stronger woman of God. I know now that I have a purpose, and it is to serve people. I get to go out five days a week, taking food to hundreds of families. I now have a personal relationship with many of them. We pray together, and I tell them about salvation in Jesus. I look forward to seeing them as much as they look forward to seeing me!"

I think about Joyce's story—and thousands of stories as miraculous as hers—whenever I remember my nights in the Dairy Queen parking lot, out east of LA on the 10 freeway.

I could have quit that first night—or on so many other nights—and driven home to Phoenix. Knowing the family I have and the connections I had in Phoenix, going home probably would have worked out fine for me.

But what about Joyce Dunigan? What if there had been no place for her to find help when she was down to her last options?

That's the thing about quitting. It doesn't only affect you. In fact, if you don't quit, if you give God twenty-four more hours and hang in there, people around you will be encouraged to trust God and hang on. And people you meet in the future will also be encouraged to go on, because you went on . . .

> because you stayed with a tough ministry,
> because you held on through a difficult season in
>   your marriage,

because you kept praying for that unsaved loved one,
because you gave God time to change your
     situation—or to change you.

In fact, if we could look ahead in time and catch a glimpse of the big picture, we would see kids, grandkids, and great grandkids someday feeling the impact of whether we throw in the towel or trust the Lord for another twenty-four hours, whether we keep stumbling on for a few more steps, or quit now.

But here is a bit of encouragement: once you face several quitting points in your life and overcome them, God begins to give you a vision of the finish line. I know that because I went eyeball-to-eyeball with Him in enough of those Dairy Queen moments to have settled the issue in my heart once and for all. I have told God, "Unless You move me from this place, I'm here for keeps."

I know very well that I will have good times, I will have dark times, and I will have a few *very* dark times. But it doesn't matter because I have already committed myself to reaching the finish line.

If you don't quit,
if you give God
twenty-four more
hours and hang
in there, people
around you will
be encouraged
to trust God
and hang on.

No, God won't always give you a vision of the finish line.

But He will always give you a vision of your next step.

Take that step, and you will be one step closer to fulfilling God's dream for your life.

"Where Do I Find the Strength?"

WHEN YOU ARE A HUSBAND AND A FATHER OF seven and living on the margin, losing your job is something more than an inconvenience.

It's sheer disaster.

For Joel Guzman, a young man with a strong work ethic who loves his family, the loss of his job was a nightmare that kept getting worse. He had proudly established himself in his job, had found an adequate rental house for his family, and had a functional car. Life wasn't anything fancy, but he felt good knowing that he was taking care of his loved ones. He was a provider, and there is great dignity in that.

But then, with absolutely no warning, Joel got a pink slip. He looked and looked, but he couldn't find work anywhere. And the Guzmans' secure little world began to unravel.

"We tried to keep up with the rent on my wife's salary," he recalls, "but it just wasn't enough. We ended up going to CalWORKs (a welfare program of Los Angeles) for assistance. They told us about some low-income housing options, but there was a waiting list. Getting a place could take up to a year.

"But if we became *homeless*, they told us, we would be moved up to the top of the list as an emergency case."

The state was encouraging the Guzmans to become homeless?! With seven kids? Joel's stomach churned. Bad things happened to people living on the streets.

After the family spent a scary, distressing week out on Skid Row, Joel went back to CalWORKs hoping that they had found a place for his family. But the social worker had bad news: there were no more low-income housing options. In fact, that program had closed. They could put the Guzmans up in a motel for fourteen days, but that was it. After those two weeks, CalWORKs could do nothing more for the family.

———

On Day 13, Joel had been out looking for work—just as he had every day—with no success.

And he was praying.

That's when an odd thought came into his mind: "Take your family on a bus ride." So the whole Guzman tribe loaded onto a metro bus, but even Joel himself wasn't sure where they were headed.

"We were on a bus going down Alvarado Avenue," Joel recalls. "I was wondering what in the world we were going to do. What would happen to us out on the streets? Would the authorities take our kids away? Just after we passed the Hollywood Freeway, my hand reached up and pulled the buzzer for the next stop. I wondered, *Why in the world did I do that? Why am I stopping here?*"

Getting out on the corner of Alvarado and Kent,

Joel and his family found themselves looking across the street at the campus of the Dream Center. Initially, they thought it was some kind of church outreach, and Joel reasoned that they might be able to get another hotel voucher to stave off disaster a little longer.

At that time, however, our rooms were filled to capacity. There was simply no spot for a family of nine, but we took Joel's number and said we would call as soon as something opened up. Joel's wife began to weep. The family wandered into a nearby store, just looking around, trying to figure out what to do next. Joel gathered his family around him and led them in prayer.

Then Joel's cell phone rang. A room had just opened up. The Guzmans could be admitted immediately.

"The Dream Center took us in, the whole family, and gave us a clean, safe place to stay. I don't know how to explain it. It's like we were at home. We felt such peace in our hearts. It helped me to trust God with our lives once again, knowing that He would help us find the right path."

Joel would need that assurance, because his wife decided "she wanted to live her own life"—a life that

Joel was
surrounded by
many people
who were seeing
miracles in their
lives, so Joel
turned to the
Lord instead
of giving up
in despair.

didn't include Joel or the seven children. And she simply walked out of their lives. Joel was surrounded by many people who were seeing miracles in their lives, so Joel turned to the Lord instead of giving up in despair. Joel also knew that he had seven sets of eyes on him: each child was looking to him to step up and be a dad. "I turned more and more to God for knowledge and understanding of the whole situation," he says. "It didn't make much sense to me, but I just had to fall back on the fact that God knew what He was doing."

In the book of Psalms, David wrote these words:

> *God is our refuge and strength,*
>   *always ready to help in times of trouble.*
> *So we will not fear when earthquakes come*
>   *and the mountains crumble into the sea.*
> *Let the oceans roar and foam.*
>   *Let the mountains tremble as the waters surge!*
> PSALM 46:1–3 NLT

At times Joel felt as if the earth were quaking and the mountains were falling into the sea. At times he still does.

"Sometimes I think about the situation and get scared. Taking care of seven kids by myself? It's overwhelming. That's when I run to my place of peace and tranquility: the Word of God. When my kids take their naps or do homework, I take advantage of the quiet time and open up my Bible. I enjoy just getting lost in the words of my heavenly Father. I pray, I meditate on those words, and I remind myself of all the positive things in my life.

"I know God isn't done with me yet. I believe I still have bigger things to accomplish for His kingdom. We've lost everything for a reason."

I find Joel's faith incredibly encouraging.

To lose his job, lose his home, lose his wife, to be left with no prospects for employment or housing and seven kids ranging in ages from seven to seventeen seems like a tragedy of almost Job-like proportions. But Joel has placed his life and the lives of his children into the hands of the living God. And in the few quiet moments of his day when the kids are asleep, Joel loses himself in talking to the Lord and meditating on His Word. And renewed hope comes.

———————

A number of years ago, a CNN program host interviewing Billy Graham asked, "What is the most difficult thing for you to do in your Christian life?"

Dr. Graham answered: "To pray."

What an honest answer!

I think Satan's first priority is to take us believers away from prayer, to separate us from the Source of our strength and help, and to put us under the weight of our burdens and circumstances, which none of us are equipped to bear.

In the Psalms, David said, "God is our refuge and strength, always ready to help in times of trouble. So we will not fear" (Psalm 46:1–2 NLT). If our adversary can somehow separate us from our only Source of strength, he has achieved his major objective in our life.

People allow time to pass without praying, and the

more time that passes, the easier it becomes to let even more time pass. And then they begin to say to themselves, "Well, if it's been this long since I sought the face of God, why even try now?" They begin to feel distant from God, imagining they have drifted too far away to overcome that separation. They say, "I have so much ground to make up before I can get back in touch with God, why even bother trying now?"

Our God, however, is the God of the *now*. He is the God of the present. And He will respond to those who turn to Him in faith. Many people I've talked to, however, feel that God must be keeping score and that He will only listen to them if they have crossed all their t's, dotted all their i's, and have been consistent in their prayer time. Not true! He will respond anytime and every time.

I sometimes hear people say, "Why should I start praying now when I've never prayed before?" Or maybe, "When I get myself together, then I'll go to church." But then they never seem to get themselves together!

As you probably already know, the biggest battle of your life will always be making time to be with God.

I think Satan's first priority is to take us believers away from prayer, to separate us from the Source of our strength and help, and to put us under the weight of our burdens and circumstances, which none of us are equipped to bear.

Why? Because during that time we connect with Him who is our Power Source. That time you spend with God is the light switch. That's also when you can slow down, listen, and learn His dreams for you.

The bottom line here? With God in your life, there is always hope!

How Desperate Are You for God?

People who have led privileged, mostly insulated lives have a Plan A . . . with Plans B, C, and D in their back pockets just in case.

In a time of crisis, they have options. Contingency plans. Choices.

Even when the bottom drops out of their life, they usually land on their feet.

In my life, I have a great marriage and two kids who love their daddy. I grew up in a strong Christian home, in a large, loving church, and in a community of people who knew me and cared about me. I have a family heritage of people who know and love God's Word. Even before I was married, I always knew in the back of my mind that if for some reason I didn't make it in LA, I could always go back to Phoenix. At any point in time I could pack it in, go home, get some R&R, fatten up on my mom's good cooking, and then think about starting something new.

Many of the people we work with, however, have no Plan B; they have absolutely no fallback option. When the bottom falls out for them, they don't land on their feet. But *they land on God.* Period. They realize the only thing they have to trust in is the claim that God's Word is true, and with nowhere else to go, they choose to believe it with all their hearts.

The fact is, however, many of them have had to swim through the deep end of hell to get to Jesus.

I think of my friend Kimmie Snowbarger.

———

Kimmie and her older sister, Brittany, are dynamos for Jesus. They remind me of those big turbines under

Hoover Dam, spinning and spinning—and overflowing with power and energy.

It wasn't that long ago, however, when the girls didn't even believe in God. They had been using drugs most of their lives, and they were in and out of trouble for as long as they could remember.

Kimmie, who was facing jail time before she came to us, was so violent that she beat up everyone she met at juvenile hall. She was addicted to both meth and heroin, and she had crammed a lifetime of bad experiences into her eighteen years.

"I grew up in Simi Valley, California, in a broken, unstable home," Kimmie explains. "My dad left my mom when I was little. He was highly addicted to crack, cocaine, and crystal meth. When I was seven, my mom remarried my little brother's dad, and I called him 'Dad' for the next seven years. He was an abusive man in every way—mentally, physically, and verbally. I witnessed a lot of domestic violence in those years before my mom finally divorced him."

He wasn't the kind of man you would miss, but he had been the only father Kimmie had known. In spite of all his violence and abuse, his sudden absence left a void in her young life. At twelve years old, Kimmie felt abandoned and lonely, and she began to drink alcohol and smoke cigarettes and marijuana. In tenth grade, she dropped out of school. By age fourteen, she was shooting up and highly addicted to heroin.

As these stories so often go, that's about the time when she linked up with a hateful, violent man who made her life much worse. "When I was sixteen, I got into a very abusive and controlling relationship. I became pregnant, but I knew that I wanted drugs more than a baby, so I got an abortion. When that relationship ended, my addiction went to the next level, and I began to inject crystal meth and heroin at the same time."

By this time Kimmie had met up with her real father, and they, along with her sister, Brittany, began shooting up together. And where did she find the money to support such vicious addictions?

"I did a lot of crime," Kimmie recalls. "I was selling drugs, breaking into homes, and stealing wherever and whatever I could." Finally apprehended, she was sent to juvenile hall. People kept their distance from her, knowing her to be extremely violent and ready to explode at a moment's notice.

It seemed as if Kimmie had hit bottom. And just when it seemed that life couldn't get much worse, her little family was invaded by . . . heaven.

———

Someone had invited Kimmie's dad, a nominal Muslim, to Angelus Temple, where he found Jesus Christ as his Savior. Soon after that, Kimmie's older sister Brittany entered our treatment program, and she too found Christ.

"My big sister wrote to me while I was in juvie," Kimmie says. "She told me she wanted me to come to the Dream Center and be with her. She also told me how the Center had changed her life."

Released from juvenile hall, Kimmie visited us on a bright, sunny day in January.

"I was really high when I arrived, and Dad and Brittany tricked me into filling out an application, which I really hadn't intended to do."

Two days after that, Kimmie's mom kicked her out of the house, and she was apprehended by authorities and jailed again for another crime.

Kimmie begged the judge to send her to the Dream Center instead of prison, and the judge relented. Kimmie was required to attend our program, but she had no desire at all to change her life. She just wanted a ticket out of jail.

On January 26, 2012, Kimmie walked through our doors. But it didn't work out the way she thought.

———

Instead of pretending to respond to the message of the gospel until she could get out again and go back to her old lifestyle, Kimmie actually leaped to receive Jesus Christ.

"Since I've been here, I've made God the center of my world. I've been completely transformed. The whole setup started as a joke to me, but it isn't anymore. I've been completely freed from addiction, anger, anxiety, trust issues, and separation anxiety. I know that I'm not alone anymore. God's been with me through it all. I can put all my trust in Him and not be scared, because I know He is faithful."

What's so stunning to Kimmie is that she finds herself with the family life she never had before. Her dad had left her when she was a little girl, and her big sister was basically lost to her too, strung out on drugs, absorbed in her own addictions and troubles. And then they were together again, but only to do drugs together, to shoot up together, and together they slipped further and further into the darkness of addiction and crime.

Now, together again under one roof, a dad and his two daughters are sober, transformed inside and out, and worshiping and serving the Lord together.

At this writing, Kimmie has just received her GED after pursuing the high school education she had never finished. And now, for the first time ever, she has begun to dream about a secure, happy future.

"I'm not a dope-sick junkie anymore."

Kimmie chooses her next words carefully, a sense of wonder in her voice. "I have a light about me now. It's . . . it's something that I've never had before. God is so real to me. And I'm so thankful that He chose me."

A broken family. A mom who threw her out. Distant memories of an absent dad. Not-so-distant memories of a violent, abusive stepdad. A controlling, angry boyfriend. Kimmie didn't have much to fall back on. But she has been making some new and happy family memories, and she continues to hold on to Jesus with everything in her. And He holds on to her—and He will never let her go (Romans 8:38–39)!

Kimmie's story isn't at all like mine.

Because of my own wonderful family with its rich Christian heritage, there are certain things that I, Matthew Barnett, have never experienced in my life, and I probably never will. I have never been hooked on drugs or, for that matter, even tried marijuana. I've never been addicted to alcohol or tangled up with pornography. I've never been drunk or stoned. I've never been in jail except as a visitor. I've never lived on Skid Row, I've never hired a prostitute, and I've never been part of a gang.

Yet just like everyone else, I am capable of any of

these things. And just like everyone else, I need to be on my guard. Bottom line, however, there is a bunch of stuff I've never done, and I'm grateful.

But does that track record, then, define my life? Is that track record the measure of my spirituality? Am I, as a Christian, the sum of what I *haven't* done? Is that what a Christian is? Is that a person who goes to the head of God's line, receives a gold star on His heavenly chart, and gets a friendly, indulgent pat on the back by an angel or two?

I really don't think so. That's not what I see in the pages of God's Word. I think the real question is *How desperate am I for God right now?* Do I cling fervently to His promises like Kimmie, Brittany, and their dad did? How eagerly and gratefully do I seek God's presence? How often do I throw myself at the altar of His grace, pleading with Him to help me, protect me, and change me?

I think that those of us who have grown up in Christian homes, with all the advantages of love and security and good teaching, need to be careful about congratulating ourselves too much. We need to be cautious about patting ourselves on the back for living a fairly clean life and not becoming swallowed up in this or that sin. No, perhaps we never became a drug addict or a prostitute or a thief. But the people who do will often fall on the Lord's mercy and cling to Him with all their might—and they just may be in line before those of us who have become smug or complacent in our cautious, careful lives.

———

Jesus once shocked the Pharisees right down to their sandals by saying to them, "Truly I tell you, the tax collectors and the prostitutes are entering the kingdom of God ahead of you" (Matthew 21:31 NIV).

The truth is, God zeros in on a hungry heart like a laser beam. One time, for instance, Jesus found a little man named Zacchaeus sitting up in a tree. This hated and despised tax collector was utterly scorned by the whole respectable, religious community of his day. But Jesus was drawn to the man's hungry heart. Zacchaeus had tossed aside his dignity and climbed a tree in order to get a better view of the Lord as He went by. And Jesus said to him, in effect, "That's the kind of desire I will always reward. I choose to have dinner with *you*."

For many people who have lived at the Dream Center, life becomes pretty simple.

Jesus. Family. The Bible. Brothers and sisters in Christ. Not too much else. As someone recently expressed it to me, "It's beans, rice, and Jesus Christ!"

The first thing people have to trust when they enter one of our programs is the process of transformation. We make that clear right up front. So they commit themselves to the spiritual disciplines of reading God's Word and prayer—a step out in faith that God will do in their lives the work He says He will do.

So these people talk to God, look to their leaders for structure and encouragement, and hold on to God's promises like a scuba diver twenty fathoms under the ocean holds on to his air hose. The Bible isn't just a book; it is *life* itself.

And that's why worship services and Bible studies

are so fun and exciting around the Dream Center. When our students turn in their Bibles to this page or that, they start getting excited even while they're still flipping the pages. Why? Because they know God will have something special for them. They don't even know what the verse they're turning to is going to be. They're just convinced that the moment they get there, they will find a life-changing word for them.

And funny thing. It usually is.

Not long ago I was thinking about these very different walks of faith in the context of a football game.

Many people I've worked with in recovery begin their life in Christ at the one-yard line. They've had no biblical teaching, no church background, no Christian heritage, and few, if any, positive role models—much less Christian role models—in their life. And then they come to Christ, and in time they move all the way up to the fifty-yard line. Others of us, however—those of us with a lifetime of godly training, encouragement,

In one sense poverty or other crushing circumstances in life can be a blessing: *they reveal that we really have no fallback option other than Jesus.*

teaching, and help—start at the fifty-yard line and maybe make it all the way to the thirty- or the twenty-five-yard line before we die.

Who has gone the farthest? Those people with no background may not be as far down the field as I am, but in light of where they started, they've actually covered more yards than I ever will. The question isn't "Where did you start in your Christian journey?" but "How far have you advanced?"

I am constantly challenged by people in our recovery program who cling to God's Word with all their heart and soul, who hang on with fingernails and toenails, because they have no other option. I hear testimonies from people who have jumped into the deep end, literally trusting God with their very life. Their example is a rebuke to those of us who have become too complacent, too self-sufficient, and too satisfied with the current level and temperature of our faith.

This may sound strange, but that's why in one sense poverty or other crushing circumstances in life can be a blessing: *they reveal that we really have no fallback option other than Jesus.* How do we wake up to the fact that there really is no other choice, that there really is no other way to do life? There is no second solution or Plan B. We don't like to think about it, but the only way some of us come to such a realization is through difficult trials that knock the false foundations out from under our feet.

Whoever we are, whatever our background, and however we may have been raised, each one of us needs an active trust in God. *Trust* is a verb! We simply get on our knees and ask God to help us rely on Him and on Him alone. We get up each morning, think about the promises of God, and hold on to them with all our hearts.

Beyond that, those of us who have been saved for a long time need to be around people who are newly saved. These men and women are often living every waking moment very much in the presence of God and participating in the spiritual disciplines, and they sharpen everyone around them, me included. Yes, I have more of a foundation in Christ than they do, but I will be honest with you: I'm constantly being slapped upside the head by their freshness, their joy, their love, and their fire.

When I walk the floors and see young women like Kimmie who have had such unbelievably broken lives and have been so completely transformed, it's almost hard for me to believe sometimes. I see them out in the parking lot at 5:30 in the morning, praying over people's cars and asking God's blessing on the people who drive them. I see them in the kitchen, so full of joy that they can't wait to wash dishes or scrub the floor or make a salad or do their next chore for the Lord. They can't wait to go to Bible study, can't wait to give their testimony, can't wait for the next worship service.

And God . . . He can't wait to be with them either.

He will move heaven and earth to be with anyone whose heart is hungry for Him.

And that's when He begins to reveal His dreams.

He will move
heaven and
earth to be
with anyone
whose heart
is hungry
for Him.

"There Has to Be Something More!"

W HEN FOURTEEN-YEAR-OLD DALLAS CAME HOME from school one afternoon, his mother thought he looked a little bit depressed.

"Here," she said, handing him a smoke. "Try this."

He did. It was crystal meth, and just that quickly Dallas became a very young addict. He smoked meth through much of his fourteenth year. What he remembers most about the experience was how it seemed to amplify everything—including his anger, his loneliness, his frustration, and his hatred.

"I turned to the first people who would accept me—and it was the kids who used drugs and partied all the time."

When Dallas was four, both of his parents were arrested and sent to prison on theft and methamphetamine charges, and Dallas was thrown into the foster care system. He didn't get to see his sister for a year because the system kept them apart.

"My grandma adopted me, my sister, and one of my brothers about a year later, and things began to look up a little. My sister and I both struggled with lots of anger, and we were having difficulty in school, but it was better than it had been," Dallas recalls. "My grandma even tried to get us going to church."

When Dallas was eight, however, life took another sharp turn for the worse. "My older brother started to sexually molest me. And he molested me for nearly a year. That really broke me, because it messed up my mind, and I didn't know who I was. I wanted acceptance, but I was so ashamed of what had happened to me. I kept trying to convince myself that it was all just a bad dream. Finally, I turned to the first people who would accept me—and it was the kids who used drugs and partied all the time. So I started hanging out with them, doing all the stuff they were doing. Drinking, smoking weed, partying, and fighting."

Back with his mother at age fourteen, Dallas began his addiction to meth and found that the drug amplified the dark areas in his mind and heart.

"I hated everyone around me, and I alienated myself from everyone. Mostly, I hated myself and all the fakeness of my life. I didn't know who I was, but I couldn't stand not being myself."

Arrested for his crimes, Dallas was sentenced to six months in a juvenile prison camp in northern California. While he was there, he encountered some people he couldn't figure out.

"There was this Christian group that would come up every Sunday, and they loved on us. To me, it didn't make any sense. I remember thinking, *How can they love me for no reason? What makes them so different, that they can love so freely?*"

When a man gave his testimony about being sexually molested as a child, Dallas could hardly believe his ears. *How can he tell us this?* he wondered. *How can he be so free about this and so open? What makes him so different from me?*

Dallas began to consider the possibility that there

really might be a God. But then he got released and remembered thinking, *Maybe there's a God, and maybe there's not. But right now I gotta worry about me.*

Ironically, Dallas ended up getting a job as a drug counselor . . . in the same probation office that had arrested him. He took on the role as a teaching assistant at his school, he had a girlfriend, and life began to take on some normalcy.

Except for one thing.

———

Dallas was sixteen years old, and he felt completely empty inside. The anger, hatred, and addictions were gone, but so was everything else. He felt like an empty shell. Like an abandoned house with no light in the windows.

That's when he decided he would take a chance on praying.

"I remember saying, 'There just has to be something more than this. God, if You're real, then just let me know *right now.*'"

That's when Dallas got the greatest surprise of his young life.

God answered him.

"I felt Him in my heart," Dallas remembers. "And He was like, 'I want you to go to the Dream Center.'"

It was a big decision for a young man to make all by himself, but that's exactly what Dallas did. He quit his job, ended his relationship, and entered our Teen Discipleship rehab program.

During that year, Dallas found the answer to his biggest, most crushing need: filling the emptiness—that vast void of nothingness—at the core of his soul. Jesus filled up that hole with Himself, filled it to the brim and then to overflowing.

After many years of unhappiness, anger, and confusion, Dallas Doty had a wonderful seventeenth year of life. "I had lots of alone time with God," he explains, "and I also had some great leaders pouring discipline and structure into my life. They modeled how to have a servant's heart. It really shaped who I am today."

Now at age eighteen, Dallas has been an intern here for two years. Through his work in the children's ministry, he is reaching hundreds of kids who began their lives much like he did. Everyone who comes in contact with Dallas is touched by his seemingly tireless work ethic and his infectious kindness.

His sister, Diamond, is also here, and they have become closer than ever. She has graduated from our Teen Discipleship rehab program. But Diamond and her husband will soon be moving on . . . to open a brand-new Dream Center on the Jersey Shore.

"I help run the children's ministry and the dance team, and I also cover shifts in the café when they're overworked.

"It's a great life," Dallas says with a smile. "I guess you could say I'm addicted to the ministry here. I can't see myself doing anything else."

Dallas has learned that just as the methamphetamines of his early days would amplify the darkness, anger, and fear in his heart, his relationship with Jesus has amplified the light and joy.

"I love my life," he says simply.

Dallas has learned that just as the methamphetamines of his early days would amplify the darkness, anger, and fear in his heart, his relationship with Jesus has amplified the light and joy.

And for those who know where Dallas came from, those four words point to nothing less than a miracle.

———

When he was a young teenager, Dallas had felt charred from the inside out, charred by his broken family, his helpless rage, and his extensive use of alcohol, marijuana, and meth. Even later, when he enjoyed good health, a girlfriend, a job, and freedom from prison, he couldn't escape feeling hollow, empty, and without purpose.

That's when Dallas did an experiment: he called on God. Did the Lord have an antidote for Dallas's feelings of desolation and futility?

It turned out that He did.

Every one of us faces such times in life, when our dreams have drained away, when we feel like a robot just going through the motions. That's why Dallas's story is so important. He was bold enough to ask God to show up in his life, to step into that emptiness. And God did.

If Dallas Doty were with you right now, he would flash one of his infectious smiles at you and say, "Give it a try."

What's Holding You Back?

IMAGINE HOLDING A SLINGSHOT.

Firmly gripping your weapon in one hand, you pull back the elastic band with the other hand as far as you can, past your ear, almost to the breaking point.

And then . . . you just let go.

The sudden release of all that pent-up energy sends the stone far, far away.

That is a picture of forgiveness.

And forgiveness is both a powerful dynamic and a wonder to behold. In my eighteen years of ministry, forgiveness may be the most potent spiritual force I have ever witnessed.

A scientist who studied the physics of a common

slingshot pointed out that all the energy stored in the elastic band, stretched to its maximum, is suddenly transferred to the stone as kinetic energy. The released stone carries away every bit of the energy that was once stored in the band.[1]

And maybe, just maybe, the giant you were aiming at will then come crashing to earth like a fallen redwood.

I'm a pastor, and I don't know all that much about physics, but I do know this: when wounded, discouraged, embittered, and greatly wronged men, women, and teens finally choose to let go of old hatreds, resentments, anger, and bitterness toward those who have so deeply hurt and misused them, something powerful happens.

I call it "reverse momentum." It's almost as though the very power that was holding them back from forgiving and creating such great stress and negative energy, now thrusts them forward, freeing them to walk with

Christ with renewed energy and passion. The tables are suddenly turned and all of that negative power starts flowing in the opposite direction—a positive, healing power replaces the wounding, crippling influence of the unforgiveness that pulled them back and held them down.

Forgiveness is nothing less than a reversal of life's momentum, and I have seen it more times than I can count.

———

I think of my young friend Angel Villarreal. You might not imagine that a teenager would have that much negative momentum to reverse. But Angel has seen more of the dark side of life in his seventeen years than many people see in seventy.

"Everybody I have ever known has let me down, stabbed me in the back, or broken my heart in one way or another," Angel tells people when he shares his testimony. "I came to the point where I lost all control of myself and gave up on life. I started drinking every day, and I got introduced to the wonderfully awful world of pills and cocaine. I became suicidal, and I cut myself a lot. I always told myself I was going to end it all, and I tried a few times. But something always saved me. I kept selling drugs and doing anything and everything I could to get them. I lived high. There was never a moment when you could have caught me sober.

"So I had really bad trust issues when I came here to the Dream Center. I didn't really want to talk to anyone, and I wasn't going to trust anyone."

But Angel had no other choice but to enter our recovery program. Deeply enmeshed in crime and the drug culture, he was court-ordered into it. He didn't want to come, but facing up to twenty years in prison on adult charges, he thought the Dream Center might be a better option.

Angel was a bitter young man who had suffered abuse from the adults in his life for as far back as he could remember. Understandably, he didn't have much regard for authority or authority figures. But he had never met leaders like those he encountered at the Center.

"I now have leaders in my life, people in positions of authority here, who have shown me that I can trust them. They really do care, they really will help me, and they don't judge me for anything.

"And I've learned a new term," Angel says with a shy smile. "It's *unconditional love*. I can trust these guys. No matter how many times I slip and fall, they're here to help me back up again. They don't abandon me like everybody else in my life has. I'm beginning to learn to trust people."

More importantly, Angel has learned those things and more from Jesus Himself.

"Although I've suffered a lot of hurt from a lot of people, I realize that they need forgiveness just as I do. I've already forgiven a lot of people, and the only way this is possible is through Jesus Christ. Ever since I came to God, I've been able to see beyond the current pain of this world and let go of the hurt that has been weighing me down for so long. If God can forgive all the sinners in the world, I can forgive the small number of them who have hurt me. All glory be to God. I'm moving forward."

"Ever since I came to God, I've been able to see beyond the current pain of this world and let go of the hurt that has been weighing me down for so long."

Actually, Angel has been launched forward. A talented musician, he is once again working on his skills and slowly rediscovering his dreams for the future. He wants to play guitar in a worship band and share his story with people who are just as he once was.

"I still have a lot to work on," he admits, "but I know I can do it because through Christ all things are possible." And "all things" includes the very thing that had seemed most impossible of all: rebuilding a relationship with his dad.

Thinking about the way forgiveness can reverse life's momentum, a friend likened forgiveness to jujitsu, where you use an attacker's momentum against him, throwing him down and defeating him with his own energy.

For many of the people here, forgiveness pushes the reset button of life. Once they get *that* issue resolved, they can begin to see potential in their lives.

They begin to dream again.

Sadly, however, some people simply can't bring

themselves to let go of old hurts. I'm reminded of Saul, the first king of Israel. At the last moment before his anointing, he got cold feet about becoming king and went looking for a place to hide. The search party finally found the king-elect in the baggage room, crouching under a pile of coats and suitcases.

That's a picture of the way some people react to the idea of forgiving those who hurt them. When God brings them to a moment of great opportunity and unparalleled possibility—a moment when He desires to release them from the luggage of their past and launch them into a joyful new chapter of life—they go back and hide in the old baggage. They insist on strapping on the too-heavy backpack of resentment and on dragging along the oversized, overstuffed duffels of anger, bitterness, and the desire for revenge.

No matter which recovery program you look into, unforgiveness will always be the number one roadblock. It is by far the greatest obstacle and the strongest negative force most people will face. In some ways, unforgiveness becomes an addiction more powerful than alcohol or drugs. And here is the grave danger: if a person holds on to unforgiveness long enough, it will become absorbed into their very identity, a part of who they are. In addition, unforgiveness distorts life to the point that a person begins to think, "I don't have any reason to go forward in my life, and I don't have any real hopes on the horizon. I am defined by my hurt. I am defined by the evil or injustice or unfairness I've experienced. It is who I am."

C. S. Lewis described much the same dynamic when he wrote about grumbling:

> Hell begins with a grumbling mood, always complaining, always blaming others . . . but you are still distinct from it. You may even criticize it in yourself and wish you could stop it. But there may come a day when you can no longer. Then there will be no "you" left to criticize the mood or even to enjoy it, but just the grumble itself, going on forever like a machine.[2]

In other words, if you don't release unforgiveness, sooner or later it will saturate your very identity, and you will lose personhood.

But letting go of unforgiveness is never easy.

I'm reminded of a missionary who was driving his small pickup through the streets of a Peruvian village when he saw a little old woman almost doubled over from the load of sticks she carried on her back. When he offered her a ride in his truck, she shyly accepted. After getting back on the road, however, he glanced in his rearview mirror to see the woman squatting in the back of the pickup with the heavy load of sticks still on her back. She had accepted the ride, but thought she still had to bear the weight.

There's no use getting into the back of the Lord's truck for a ride if we insist on carrying our crushing loads rather than laying them down.

Every one of us has had to deal with this issue to one degree or another. Many of us may not have suffered the terrible abuses I've described in these pages, but our unforgiveness of whatever we have experienced holds us back.

I have found the best way to help people let go of their past and forgive those who have hurt them is to simply fill their vision with Jesus. I encourage them to look at Him for who He is, see what He came to do, and learn from the radical ways He forgave others. The better we understand Jesus' nature, the better chance we have to walk in that nature.

The bottom line, of course, is that true, from-the-heart forgiveness isn't a human quality at all. Loving the people who have wounded you, neglected you, or harmed you makes no earthly sense.

That's because true forgiveness is supernatural.

In the natural realm, genuine forgiveness can't happen. It would be like a mighty river flowing backward, like a lightning bolt being absorbed by a cloud, like an avalanche roaring back up a mountainside.

Forgiveness, then, is nothing less than solid evidence of Christ's great power.

So, instead of trying hard to forgive, allow the forgiveness of Christ to flow through you like an electric current racing through a copper cable.

You will never, never be the same after that.

An Adventure Worth Living For

Our children, Mia and Caden, love nothing more than jumping aboard the food truck with me and going out to one of the many inner city sites where we serve meals.

It's more than a job. For my family, it's sheer adventure.

The kids can't wait to carry boxes, serve the food, pick up trash, and talk to the people who line up for a meal.

There was one time, however, when Mia and Caden became a little anxious.

The lines were really long that day, and after doing a quick visual inventory of what we had in the truck, they came to me with worried expressions on their little faces. "Dad! We don't have enough food. We're going to run out!"

"You just watch," I told them. "There'll be enough food."

They glanced at each other as if to say, *What is he talking about?* "But, Dad!" they protested. "We're almost out!"

"It's okay," I said. "I don't know how it will happen, but everyone is going to get fed today. There will be enough food."

And somehow there was! That little bit of food fed all those patient people waiting in line, and no one went away hungry that day. As we were packing up, the kids were wide-eyed with wonder. "Dad," they said, "that was just like the Bible story about the five loaves and the two fish!"

"That's the way it always works," I told them. "It's happened every single time, no matter how many people show up. We've never been short. We've never run out. God always comes through."

God always comes through.

That's the lesson Mia and Caden went away with that day, and I don't imagine they will ever forget it. I think that one experience impacted them far more than a hundred lectures on the bigness and faithfulness of God. They got to see God's sufficient provision first-hand while they distributed that food with their own hands.

It's one thing to help Dad with a task. It's another thing to find yourself in the middle of a miracle. Someday, when my kids find themselves facing a hard deadline, a scary medical diagnosis, a heartbreaking relationship, or a season when there's more month than paycheck, I'm guessing that they will remind themselves, *God always comes through. He's done it before, and He'll do it again. I can trust Him in this.*

———

We live in a culture today that tries to push God out of the marketplace of ideas and shut Him out of every public discussion. Many public schools don't even allow His name to be mentioned. Popular media mocks His followers, uses His name only as a swear word, and ignores the role of faith in everyday life.

Knowing that's what our children will encounter day after day, our role as parents is to show them something different.

Yes, *show*. Not just tell.

If we want our kids to have a stronger spiritual life than ours, we need to show them God's power, His faithful provision, and the extraordinary things He can do in people's lives when they submit to Him.

But no matter how well intentioned we might be, we won't successfully teach this lesson with our words alone.

———

Before Caroline and I had children, I sometimes worried about whether we would be able, on a pastor's salary, to give them the opportunities they needed to really succeed in life. Specifically, would we be able to help our kids get into the "right" schools, attend the "right" college, or find the "right" career?

After Mia and Caden came into the world, however,

and as they grew up around Angelus Temple and the Dream Center, all of those concerns melted away. I came to realize that my children's lives would be enriched to the maximum level not by money or an elite education, but rather by the life experiences we would share.

So, from the time they could toddle, my daughter and son have ministered with me. They're out with me every week, serving on the food truck, meeting and helping people in the neighborhoods, and working in the café. And they absolutely love it. The world where we minister together is a big and exciting place with lots of interesting people, scores of honorary "aunts" and "uncles," and something always happening.

Actually, what's happening most is *life*. Life out of death. Freedom out of addiction. Hope and laughter and dreams rebuilt out of wreckage and despair.

———

When I look back on my own life, I see that my dad took me on the same kind of faith adventures when I was their age.

When I wanted
to look away from
the brokenness
and poverty and
need, Dad made
me look right at
it, even when it
was difficult.

At first I felt a little shy and reluctant about interacting with needy people. I remember driving through south Phoenix when I was just a kid. We were going through a rough area, and I started to roll up my window.

My dad glanced over at me from the driver's seat. "Don't do that," he said. "I want you to keep your window open for a while. I want you to see the need that's right here in our own city."

Yes, when I wanted to look away from the brokenness and poverty and need, Dad made me look right at it, even when it was difficult. I know, without a doubt, that experiences like that one shaped me. Everything in my life and ministry today was defined by Dad exposing me to those sometimes heartbreaking experiences when he took me with him on his journey.

Yes, he paid attention to my grades and how I was getting along in school. But he was most interested in whether I was grappling with the principles of life in Christ and whether I understood what it meant to be a Christian and to serve others.

On Saturday mornings when I was just a young teenager, Dad and I would drive into some of the poorer neighborhoods of south Phoenix and park the car. "Okay, Son," he would say. "Go knock on twenty doors, and I'll knock on twenty doors. Between the two of us, we'll talk to a bunch of people about the Lord and tell them how to get rides to church."

Most of the important things I have learned in life weren't lessons from a classroom or academic circles, but rather lessons learned during family experiences and these adventures of faith with my dad.

———

Many parents wring their hands and groan, "If I could just get my kids into a better school than I went to, their lives will turn out better."

Maybe. Maybe not. That "better" school might be the worst thing that could happen to your child.

Besides, there is so much more to parenting than just providing for your kids the kind of educational or career opportunities that you didn't have. Parenting doesn't even require trying to put your kids in a position to "find security" or earn a great amount of money.

We Christians know that there are goals infinitely more important than financial goals. To be specific, what matters most is whether we are passing on a legacy of solid, scriptural values to our sons and daughters.

My dad taught me a few things that will stay with me forever. To this day I can hear him say, "Find a need and fill it. Find a hurt and heal it." But he didn't just *say* words like these, words that you'd expect a preacher to say. My dad *lived* them. And as he did, he took me along for the ride. We did ministry together. We helped hurting people together. He even took me into some of the tough meetings he had as head pastor, so I could see how a Christian leader responds under criticism and pressure.

Dad let us kids serve right alongside him, so that we could experience making a difference together, and that's what Caroline and I are trying to do with our children too.

I think the best and most blessed thing we can do for our sons and daughters is to give them opportunities to share the burdens and touch the hearts of others. It's always fun for a child to get toys, but it's even m exciting when they choose to give those same toys away to children who have nothing at all.

———————

All kinds of kids come to our children's church on a Sunday. Some parents drive their kids in from the suburbs, and other boys and girls come from South Central LA or right off Skid Row.

Some of these children are homeless, and they have never been to church in their lives. A few of them come through the doors looking a little wide-eyed and afraid. That's when my nine-year-old daughter Mia jumps in. Mia feels like it's her job to love on kids like that, to help them to feel welcome and accepted. She's always going through her stuff saying, "I'm going to give this away." She goes into that 11:00 a.m. children's church with a missionary mind-set: she wants to reach those kids who have experienced great sadness, trauma, and disappointment in their short lives.

I don't know what Mia will do when she grows up. But I am confident that, from a very young age, she's known what it means for the Lord to use her in the lives of others. That discovery will stay with her long after many of the sermons and Sunday school lessons have faded away.

My friend Brittany Giarusso grew up in the same town and attended the same church I did. She attended Christian schools and had a strong spiritual foundation early in life. But when she was a young teenager, her parents divorced, and her secure little world began to crumble. As she describes it, "I really went off on a side street . . . for a long, long time."

Brittany lost her virginity at age fourteen and had an abortion. That experience sent her even deeper into hopelessness. By the time she was in high school, she had given herself completely to the party scene: she was smoking cigarettes, drinking, smoking weed, and hanging around gangs.

"I ended up meeting a guy and getting into a long-term relationship. I got pregnant again and had my wonderful son."

For her baby's sake, Brittany tried to return to the secure life she had known as a little girl, but she just couldn't seem to find it. That search for security was like trying to unscramble the eggs in an omelet.

Depressed and filled with regrets, she began taking painkillers to numb the emotional pain. But that step only led her into deeper and even more vicious addictions.

"I just lost myself in those days," she relates. "I got into selling drugs, stealing cars, robbing people, and dealing counterfeit money. Soon I was dealing heroin—and I ended up being my own best customer. I turned into someone I couldn't even recognize, and I had to ask my mom to care for my son, because I didn't want him around my lifestyle.

"I wanted to get clean. For my son's sake, I *tried* to get clean. But nothing ever worked, and I only got worse and worse. I ended up overdosing two weeks before my twenty-first birthday. All I remember is waking up somewhere in the dark. I didn't know where I was, I didn't know where I had been, and I didn't know what I was doing. But something happened in that dark place.

"You can practice religion all you want, but if you're not applying all that God teaches you and if you're not living in the joy He gives, you're never going to have a stable foundation."

"I started thinking about God and my salvation, and a song about Jesus came into my head. I finally called my pastors in Phoenix and asked if they could get me into the Dream Center. I've been here for about a year, and a major restoration is taking place. I want my son to see that. I want him to grow up knowing that Jesus is the Way, the Truth, and the Life. I want him to know that true happiness and joy only come from living for the Lord."

Brittany understands that just talking about God to her son won't cut it. She knows that in order to influence her boy, she needs to live the life—live the miracle—right in front of his eyes.

"I was raised in church," she remembers, "and I went to church all the time. I practically grew up in Christian schools. But somehow that faith never seemed real to me. *Christian* was just a title, not a life. Now that I have that life, that's what I want for my son too.

"Also, it maybe sounds strange, but I'm actually thankful for everything I've done and everything I've seen, because the knowledge I've gained can help me keep my son from going down that path.

"The answer isn't religion; it's having a relationship with God that makes a world of difference. You can practice religion all you want, but if you're not applying all that God teaches you and if you're not living in the joy He gives, you're never going to have a stable foundation."

As time goes on, Brittany will learn how to encourage and celebrate every tentative step and every minor victory as her little boy begins to live out his own adventure of faith.

I can't tell you how much I love that phrase *adventure of faith.* If we can open our children's eyes to the reality that walking with Jesus is an exciting quest, a daily voyage toward unknown perils as well as rewards, our kids just may keep their feet on the narrow and right pathway.

No, there are no guarantees. But we will have passed on the only legacy that counts.

What to Do When You Fail

I CAN'T COUNT ALL THE WAYS WE HAVE FAILED here at the Center. Bottom line, you name it, and we've failed at it.

We have failed in our mission. We have failed to reach our goals. We have failed in our progress. We have failed in our fund-raising. We have failed in our public relations. We have failed in personnel decisions. We have failed in our financial projections. We have launched programs that never got off the ground. We've launched other programs that took off like a rocket and then promptly crash-landed.

Even so, we keep trying because we know that we are where God wants us to be, doing what He wants us to do. And we will keep stumbling along until He gives us different instructions.

I remember in the early days when we started a little recovery home in an apartment across the street from the church building I had inherited. The plan was that I would meet with the guys, open up my Bible, and just talk to them informally and from the heart. I see in retrospect that this wasn't the best plan, so no wonder it didn't always work out. But we knew that the Lord had called us to do what we were doing, so we just kept trying, kept working at it, kept refining, and kept growing through all our trials.

And our little recovery home got better and better.

Proverbs 24:16 says that "though the righteous fall seven times, they rise again" (NIV). You really don't know what's going to happen the next time you fall down and pick yourself up out of the mud. This not knowing is exactly why you have to keep getting back up again and getting back into the race. God may have something big for you just beyond that next try, that next attempt.

You really don't know what's going to happen the next time you fall down and pick yourself up out of the mud. This not knowing is exactly why you have to keep getting back up again and getting back into the race.

Believe this: there is always life after setbacks—even after a whole string of them! I think too many people imagine they have to get something right the first time. They have to have the perfect plan executed in the perfect way—and have it right now. And when that plan doesn't work out exactly the way they imagined, they're done.

I can easily identify with the prophet Jeremiah, who tried to submit his letter of resignation to the Lord on more than one occasion. Jeremiah didn't feel cut out to be a prophet, he didn't enjoy the confrontation with his stubborn, cynical countrymen, and he hated having everyone oppose him and make fun of him. I'm sure there were times when he wanted to be eloquent, but all he could do was weep. He expressed his frustration to the Lord with these words:

> I have to give them your messages because you are stronger than I am, but now I am the laughingstock of the city, mocked by all. You have never once let me speak a word of kindness to them; always it is

disaster and horror and destruction. No wonder they scoff and mock and make my name a household joke. And I can't quit! For if I say I'll never again mention the Lord—never more speak in his name—then his word in my heart is like fire that burns in my bones, and I can't hold it in any longer. (Jeremiah 20:7–9 TLB)

Jeremiah didn't quit, and God went on to use him at a moment when the fate of his nation hung in the balance. And here we are still reading about what Jeremiah accomplished some twenty-five hundred years later.

The battle is not about perfecting everything immediately. The battle is about determining the direction God has called you to go and staying the course until He tells you otherwise. As you fight the battle, realize not only that you're going to change and grow and learn, but also that God will teach you and lead you through the steps—and through the missteps as well.

Another reason people want to give up is because they don't feel acknowledged or appreciated. Nobody speaks about or honors what they do, and it seems like nobody really cares. They ask themselves, *Why should I keep trying?*

Years ago I had to wrestle with this issue. I'd worked so hard, and it seemed like nobody noticed or cared. I was telling the Lord about it because at the time He seemed to be the only One listening.

I was tabulating all my travel, my heavy fund-raising schedule, and my having to be away so much from Caroline and the kids. "Lord," I said to Him, "sometimes I feel like people just don't appreciate me."

But then the Lord spoke to me and said, "Why are you worrying about people appreciating you? You're not doing this for *them*. You're doing this unto *Me*."

That was a message that changed my life. God was saying to me, "Get back up, learn the right lessons, do the work I've given you—and do it for Me in My name, and you will never struggle with feeling unappreciated again. In fact, you will be motivated for the rest of your life."

Here is what I have realized: Everything I get from

people—every pat on the back, every encouraging word, every warm-and-fuzzy compliment, every endorsement—is just a bonus. It's a handful of change in the tip jar. And I'll take it! If people want to encourage me, wonderful! God bless 'em. *But I don't live for it.*

If you and I can keep in mind that everything we do in these terribly short lives of ours is "unto the Lord," then we will never quit, never turn back, and never run from our destiny. Whenever we feel like throwing in the towel, we're usually comparing ourselves to others rather than keeping our eyes on the Lord. I believe you and I can stay motivated forever if we stay focused on our real purpose and on who it is we really need to please.

———

In fact, when do you lose your motivation? I think it's when you begin to think about yourself and start to evaluate your life in terms of "me" and "my." When you start wondering, *What am I doing with my life?* energy and purpose begin to drain out of your days like water from a rusted-out bucket.

When do you lose your motivation? I think it's when you begin to think about yourself and start to evaluate your life in terms of "me" and "my."

Guess what? It isn't your life!

As Paul told the Christians in Rome, "None of us lives for ourselves alone, and none of us dies for ourselves alone. If we live, we live for the Lord; and if we die, we die for the Lord. So, whether we live or die, we belong to the Lord" (Romans 14:7–8 NIV).

Now I do admit that I might have an edge on you when it comes to motivation. After all, absolutely nothing will stir your faith or open your spiritual eyes or motivate you to serve God like seeing people who have given up on life come alive in Jesus, and I am privileged to see much of that. The most remarkable changes are evident in those women who have escaped the sex trade and human trafficking and come to Christ. Many of the girls who leave that sordid world and come into our program here feel like they are already dead. Some of them are indeed like walking corpses. They're just going through the motions. Life for them is only basic existence. Each of these precious women is only a burned-out shell. It's almost frightening to see their eyes—so lifeless, so empty.

But that's before Jesus begins His work.

Here on our campus, these girls find themselves

around other people who have also come through dark and terrible experiences and found life, real Life, on the other side. And as these young women realize this, that block of ice in their soul begins to melt just a little. Living in a safe place, being surrounded by people who truly care about them, and learning about a Savior who died to pay for all their sins—all this works together to rekindle their interest in life. You can see the faint but growing spark in their eyes. Sometimes almost suddenly they start seeing the possibilities of life.

They hear Jesus say, "I have come that they may have life, and that they may have it more abundantly" (John 10:10)—and they believe it! When Jesus enters their lives, it's almost like a physical shock. It's like a jumper cable has reached from the cross to their soul. It's like life for these young women begins again.

But what happens isn't like recharging a dead car battery. This awakening is like getting a whole new electrical system that has a Power Source beyond comprehension. Life begins after these girls grab hold of the live wire comprised of the grace, forgiveness, tenderness, joy, and hope of Jesus Christ.

At different points in my life when I've become discouraged or wanted to quit, the Lord has reminded me how important it is to keep trying. Not just for my own sake, but because there are other people—people I may not have even met yet—who need my perseverance, who will be encouraged by my example. There are other people I will encounter in days, weeks, and years to come who will need me to stay the course, to keep going, to keep my feet on the path. There will be people who need my journey to carry them along too.

I firmly believe this.

Consider, from the book of Psalms, the account of a man named Asaph who became discouraged and embittered about life. This man was about one inch away from walking away from everything. He wrote: "But as for me, my feet had almost slipped; I had nearly lost my foothold" (Psalm 73:2 NIV).

Living for God? What's the use? Where has it gotten me? Maybe you've asked yourself these same questions. Asaph kept talking: "Have I been wasting my time? Why take the trouble to be pure? All I get out of it is trouble and woe—every day and all day long!" (vv. 13–14 TLB).

But then it dawned on Asaph (who was a good but very discouraged man) that there were other people in his life equation besides himself. There were others who would be affected or infected by his attitude. He concluded: "If I'd have given in and talked like this, I would have betrayed your dear children" (v. 15 MSG).

If I had stopped only briefly at that Dairy Queen parking lot and then gone on home to Phoenix, if I had given up on the ministry in Los Angeles instead of turning back, how would life have been different? What would have happened to those precious young women who stepped out of hellish, dehumanizing sex trafficking and through our doors? Would someone else have ministered to them? Possibly so; but we're never allowed to see what might have been.

If I had quit and walked away in discouragement, what would have happened to my young friend Joanna Tobar?

———

Joanna grew up in Los Angeles, in Echo Park. "My father was definitely a drug addict," she recalls. "I remember seeing my mother cry because my dad wouldn't come home sometimes. Or maybe she would have to drive to some crack house to pick him up, with my little brother and sister and me in the car."

In and out of prison, enslaved by alcohol and drug habits, her dad all but faded out of their lives. Eventually, her mom left him. It was hard on all of them. He might not have been an ideal father, but he had been loving and kind in his own way, and his absence left a gaping hole.

Then came the morning when her mom took her aside and said, "We need to talk." She told Joanna that she had met someone new, that this someone would be moving in that same morning, and that this someone was another woman.

"My life was crushed into pieces," she relates in her testimony. "I felt so abandoned. I was at a crucial point in my life when I needed my mom in the worst way, and she wasn't there. But I don't blame my parents for my own destruction. I made the choice to skip school, hang out with the wrong group of friends, quit playing sports, and start drinking alcohol. I eventually dropped out of high school and started entering into very unhealthy relationships with guys."

But when Joanna was fifteen, an angel stepped into her life. This angel happened to be a real-life cousin named Angel, and he invited Joanna to play basketball with him at a place called the Dream Center.

"Back then," she remembers, "I had no idea what the Dream Center was or what it had meant for the communities of Los Angeles. But the second I heard they had a gym and you could go there and play ball—that was more than enough to get me there! I remember walking into the building and seeing all the kids in the gym, laughing, talking, and shooting baskets. There were championship banners on the walls and a snack bar. I'd never been in an atmosphere like that.

"I knew I was at the right place at the right time, because a young lady named Stella Reed introduced herself to me. Stella was a youth pastor there, and she got me connected with a team I could play on. I also got suckered into coming to a youth service on Tuesday night at the gym."

In the meantime Joanna got back in touch with her

dad, and he started coming to see her play on Friday nights. "God had this all planned out so perfectly," Joanna recalls with a smile. "Restoration was happening, and we didn't even know it. That's how cool God is! Freedom and drastic change were about to hit us in the face!"

Before long, Joanna's dad was attending the youth services with her. A man named Jason introduced himself to her dad, got to know him, and invited him to Iron Mill, a men's Bible study.

In the meantime, Joanna was getting to know her basketball coach . . . me!

"It's crazy," she says. "I didn't know who Pastor Matthew was. All I knew was that when I lost my temper in a game, he was always there to encourage and uplift me. It was something I had never really experienced in my life.

"I kept attending youth services and playing basketball, and eventually the youth leaders learned that I wasn't in school. They encouraged me to fill out an application for the Dream Center high school. I applied, was accepted, and just like that I was back in school again.

At the same time, I got a job in the coffee shop here, so I started getting work experience. It was my first job ever!"

Joanna eventually moved back in with her mom, and the two of them have hammered out a relationship. It was a lot easier for Joanna since she now had strong Christian friends and stayed away from alcohol.

In the meantime, however, her dad gave his life to Jesus Christ. "It's been so beautiful to see the transformation in my dad's life! I can honestly say he is now one of my best friends. I can't imagine doing this life without my dad!"

Joanna is now twenty-four. She graduated from high school as the class valedictorian and then began an internship at the Dream Center while she continued to work in the Terrace Café. After that year, she was accepted into The Movement, which is our leadership school. Now in her fourth year, she is overseeing the women who are in their first year of discipleship.

"It's truly an honor to play a small part in these women's lives, to see the chains broken off and watch God's transformation doing its work."

Joanna continues to pray for her mother, and she

believes that one day Jesus will change her life too. It hasn't happened yet, she acknowledges, "But it excites me to know that day is coming in His timing . . . in His perfect timing. So I will wait and trust the Lord with my whole heart, and I will continue to live life in such a way that it only encourages and honors my mom."

So what if, years ago, when I was discouraged, I had given up and abandoned the vision of reaching out to the hurt, the addicted, and the needy people living in central Los Angeles? Would someone else have developed something like the Dream Center? Would someone else have coached Joanna at that tender, pivotal moment in her young life?

Maybe. Maybe not. I'll never know.

I do know, though, that I'm glad I kept trying after so many setbacks, missteps, and failures. I'm glad I allowed the Lord to encourage my heart and keep me on track.

Because persevering wasn't just about me. It was about Joanna too.

Finding Purpose in Your Pain

STEVE FINE WAS NO AVERAGE, RUN OF THE-MILL thief. He was very good at his craft, excelling at slipping past locked doors, outwitting padlocks, and frustrating elaborate alarm systems. During his years of thievery, Steve had gained experience stealing all manner of things, large and small. As it turned out, stealing was a handy skill to have, because Steve would have some expensive addictions to finance.

How had it happened? How had he ended up in such a place in life? It wasn't because he grew up poor.

"I grew up in a wealthy home," Steve recalls, "and I never went without anything. I excelled in sports to the point that I was scouted for a professional baseball team while I was still in high school. But then I ended up getting my high school sweetheart pregnant, and I had to make a choice between playing baseball and marrying the mother of my child."

Steve got married and decided to join the Navy. He went on to become one of the Navy's most elite warriors: a SEAL. He spent eight years in the service, but when it was over, he felt utterly lost and disconnected with life.

"I was broken and angry," he remembers, "which resulted in a bitter separation from my wife. After the structured environment of the Navy, I felt like I was at loose ends, without a purpose, and now without a family. Feeling overwhelmed with life, I turned to drinking, drugs, and gangs."

And he learned how to be a thief.

Despite all his skill and daring, his crimes finally caught up with him. "I was constantly in and out of jail," he says. "After my last arrest, I was facing twenty-two years in prison."

That's when God stepped into his life in an unexpected way.

Steve's daughter Cammie, who had attended the Dream Center Teen Discipleship program years before, sent the court a petition to allow her Navy SEAL dad an opportunity to enter our men's program. After we accepted his application, the court approved of this alternative program.

In a wonderful bit of irony, Steve, the thief, had his own heart stolen by Jesus Christ. Now, several years later, he serves as the director of security for all of the $86 million Dream Center and Angelus Temple complexes. He carries keys to every lock on the entire campus, and he is the best security chief we've ever had because he knows more about breaking in and thieving than the thieves do. And no one really wants to tangle with an ex-Navy SEAL anyway!

Steve has found his purpose, and it was a purpose that grew directly out of his pain, his failures, and his mistakes.

"Since I came here," he says, "God has restored my entire life. I have been cleared of all my legal obligations, and my family is being restored. Since I came here, God has brought my other two daughters to the Dream Center along with five of my grandchildren! I get to be the spiritual leader of my family and guide them in their spiritual walk. I also went from selling drugs and stealing to maintaining the safety and well-being of all the residents. I have finally found my true purpose in life. It's to lead my family and to serve others who are in need."

I believe God loves to do exactly this kind of redeeming work in the lives of His people. I believe God loves to stand Satan's plans for evil on their head and bring great good out of them.

We can sometimes see the purpose of our pain in retrospect, in the rearview mirror, but it's not always easy to discern that purpose when we're up to our earlobes in pain and perplexity. When we're hurting or confused, it's easier to hunker down than to step out in faith.

The fact is, many people don't discover their purpose in life because they never put themselves in circumstances where God might show Himself. You don't find your purpose by hiding in the shadows, waiting for life to come to you. *Chances are, the best place to find your purpose is in the middle of someone else's pain.*

I'm reminded of a middle-aged woman who came to me for counseling.

"Pastor," she said, "I don't know what to do. I think I'm having a nervous breakdown."

"Oh?" I said.

"I want you to know that I'm a very smart woman. I have a PhD."

I nodded encouragingly.

"But I don't know what to do with myself. I've watched Oprah and Dr. Phil, and no one is able to help me."

"Well, then," I said, "I probably won't be able to help you either. But since you've come to see me, let me make a suggestion. I want you to get up tomorrow morning and bake some chocolate chip cookies. Then I want you to hand-deliver those cookies to some of the guys in our rehab program who are detoxing and getting off drugs. (Chocolate is actually very good for recovery.)

"Then the next day, I want you to do it again. Get up, bake some more cookies, and hand-deliver them to the guys in rehab. Then maybe you could take some snacks down to Skid Row and hand them out. Since nothing else is working, I think you need to try this."

The woman with the doctorate looked shocked and offended.

"Cookies?" she said. "You want me to bake *cookies*? You want me to hand out snacks to homeless people? Are you kidding me? I'm a PhD! I don't want to do that."

"I know, I know," I said. "It sounds elementary. But, really, what would it hurt? Why not give it a try?"

I quickly sketched out a seven-day plan of action for her and encouraged her to come back to see me for weekly follow-up counseling meetings. For three weeks, however, I never heard a word from her. Finally, I saw her in church and asked her how she was doing.

"Why haven't you shown up for our meetings?" I asked her. "We're supposed to talk about your nervous breakdown."

She smiled and waved me off with her hand. "Oh, Pastor," she said, "I've been so busy baking cookies and blessing people that I forgot all about my nervous breakdown!"

It was written right across her face: she had found purpose in her life by getting busy and helping people—even though she may have never baked a cookie before in her life, and it was the last thing she imagined herself doing. She was enjoying the way the faces of the men brightened up when she walked into the room and how they opened up to her when she asked how they were getting along. And she was surprised by how appreciative and friendly some of the people on Skid Row had been when she had taken them snacks.

The big deal wasn't the chocolate chip cookies. Those cookies were just the admission ticket to get her involved in people's lives.

Have you noticed a pattern? Have you seen that God works in surprising ways? He made an expert thief a director of security. He made Zacchaeus, a tax collector and thief, a generous benefactor. He made Paul, the greatest enemy and most deadly antagonist of the early church, its mightiest apostle and spokesman—a man who compared himself to a nursing mother as he cared for the people of God (1 Thessalonians 2:7).

I don't know how to explain all this except to say

that God is God and His thoughts and ideas are higher than ours—by about a billion miles. And I know that from experience.

When I first arrived in Los Angeles, a ministry of drug and alcohol rehabilitation wasn't on the short list of the things I wanted to accomplish. It wasn't on my long list either. For that matter, it wasn't on *any* list—except the one list that mattered, which was God's list. Rehab? That wasn't at all what I thought I'd been called to do! I had my five-year goals, and the Dream Center wasn't a part of any of them.

It wasn't in my plans, but it was in His plans

So often people think that their purpose in life will just fall from heaven and land at their feet or arrive in a gold-leafed envelope delivered by some heavenly UPS angel. These folks imagine that, as they sit in some comfy arm-chair, they will suddenly and clearly know everything God wants them to do.

A ministry of drug and alcohol rehabilitation wasn't on the short list of the things I wanted to accomplish. It wasn't on my long list either. For that matter, it wasn't on *any* list—except the one list that mattered, which was God's list.

But it may not happen that way. God just may want you to get your hands a little bit dirty first.

When I came here to LA, I had a strong desire to help people and make a difference in their lives. It wasn't very long before I realized that the greatest need was helping people overcome their enslaving, degrading, life-stealing addictions. I began to find my purpose in the middle of other people's pain.

How much did I know about drug and alcohol rehabilitation? *Zero.* I'd never touched drugs or alcohol in my life. And other than my excursions into south Phoenix with my dad, I'd never been around alcoholics or drug addicts. Yet now, 60 percent of my staff are graduates of drug and alcohol rehab.

It all started with a few guys sitting on folding chairs in a room at the old Bethel Temple. We wanted to start a church, but apparently God had His own ideas.

I sat there listening to them talk about the pain and wreckage in their lives because of their addictions when suddenly I surprised myself. I heard myself say, "Let's do something. Let's open up a home for drug and alcohol rehab. The Lord will help us. Let's do it!"

It was a holy moment, and I hadn't even seen it coming. But I am convinced that the reason it came was because I wanted to help people and I had made myself available to the Lord.

If our desire is to truly help people in Jesus' name, I believe we sometimes need to take that first step of faith—even if it's a baby step. I also think that there are dreams in our heart that we aren't even aware of and will only be uncovered as we step out.

That's the way we got involved in helping girls caught up in human trafficking. No one had really seen that as part of our ministry, but then . . . it landed on our doorstep.

———

One Easter Sunday we got a call from a young woman who was in a nearby motel. Her voice was frightened, desperate.

"A bunch of girls are here," she said. "A pimp has kidnapped us and is loading us up on drugs in this motel. *Can somebody come and help me?*"

Of course we sent someone over immediately, and we took this girl in. We didn't have a plan, and we really had no firm idea what to do with her except to give her a safe shelter. We said to the Lord, "God, we believe You are moving us in this direction."

Taking in that first young woman was our first step of faith, and now we have a whole floor for women rescued from human trafficking.

Our emancipated minor program started in a similar way. We got word of a young man who had been kicked out of his foster home because he'd turned eighteen, and he had nowhere to go. Too many foster parents keep the kids just to get the money from the state, and when the kids turn eighteen and there's no more money coming in, they simply put the kids out on the streets. We were feeding people on Skid Row when we found this young man, distraught, afraid, and weeping. "I have nowhere to go," he said. "I just got thrown out by my foster parents."

I remember looking at my associate and saying, "We need to help him."

"But we don't have a program for unassisted minors," he said.

"Well, we'll figure one out. Bring him in."

So now we have a program to help these young people, but that had never been part of our game plan or strategy.

The purpose rose out of need. *God-given purpose always arises out of need.*

Human need is often God's call to action.

The Dream Center is now home to many different ministries that help define our purpose, our reason to be. But we would never have uncovered those opportunities to serve if we hadn't put ourselves in a position to let our hearts be broken. Actually, we aren't doing one thing at the center that was in our original plan. In fact, the Dream Center itself wasn't in our original plan. We just showed up, and God gave us work to do.

Purposeful ministry starts with people in need, someone who has a vision for how to meet that need, and enough faith to take a step in that direction.

I can't tell you how many ministries have arisen because people recognized a need and, leaning on Jesus, moved forward to meet that need.

I can't tell you how many ministries have arisen because people recognized a need and, leaning on Jesus, moved forward to meet that need.

Not that long ago a man in our "Adopt a Block" program encountered a family with four barefoot kids. After he told me about the kids who had no shoes, he said, "Pastor, can we start a clothing store?"

"Sure," I said. "Let's go for it."

Now we have a massive clothing store on campus. It houses thousands of pieces of donated clothing—much of it brand-new, given by various companies—and huge numbers of people in our community are benefitting. It's amazing what happens when you just show up in someone's life to help meet a need.

Years ago, when my wife, Caroline, was just eighteen, she was a secretary at the center. She used to drive every day from Corona, ninety minutes away, just to be secretary at a church that served people.

One day she got a call from a woman at Social Services. "There's a very poor family down the street from the Dream Center," she said. "I was just in the home, and they're hungry. They need food. Could you deliver some?"

Caroline went to our food bank, which at that time was down to about nothing. In fact, only one bag of food was left. Caroline delivered the bag herself and knocked on the door. When the door opened, the four little kids literally tackled her and grabbed the food. They started chewing on raw zucchini as though it were the last meal they would ever have.

Their hunger shocked Caroline. These kids, just a few blocks from our church, were *starving*. Broken and shaken, she got back in her car, put her face in her hands, and wept.

When she finally lifted her face again, she wiped the tears from her eyes. And the first thing she saw was an old ice cream truck sitting across the street.

"I wonder . . ." she said to herself. "Wow! I wonder if we could transform some old ice cream trucks into mobile food banks?"

Instead of just thinking about her idea, she put legs on it. She purchased an old ice cream truck for $500 and raised the money to fix it up and refurbish it. It became our very first food truck. Now we have a number of trucks that stop at twenty-seven different sites all over Los Angeles and feed up to eight thousand people a week.

And that important outreach started when someone simply responded to a call for help, wept over the need, and took the bold step of starting to meet that need.

So many ministries, both large and small, begin when someone simply makes him or herself available. Sometimes we pray and pray and pray about finding a way to meet a particular need or solve a specific problem when the truth is, *we* are the solution.

"Why Would Anyone Believe in Me?"

Looking out my window into the twilight of a mild, spring evening, I see the two of them in our parking lot. They're laughing, talking, and high-fiving each other like a couple of old friends.

In fact, that's what they are—and they've been through a lot together.

One of them—the one with a knife-wound scar over his eye and a navy-blue Dream Center polo shirt on—is Michael Banyard. This coming Sunday he will be graduating from our discipleship/recovery program. It will be a milestone in his life: the first graduation he has ever experienced. The thin, gray-haired, seventy-something man congratulating him—this very moment as I watch—is Federal Judge Spencer Letts.

The relationship between the judge and Michael, the former convict, has been the subject of several prominent *Los Angeles Times* stories by Kurt Streeter dating back to 2010.

Michael, whom the reporter described as "a strikingly smart, sensitive man," had been addicted to drugs most of his life and ended up homeless on Skid Row. Although his rap sheet contained only relatively moderate offenses, Michael was arrested for possession of a small amount of crack cocaine in 1996 and received the mandatory sentence under California's unforgiving Three Strikes Law: twenty-five years to life.

After nine years in prison, Michael's final appeal took him into federal court where Judge Letts presided. This hearing was truly Michael's last chance. According to the *Times* article, federal judges are inundated with such appeals, and they almost never reverse convictions.

But Judge Letts did.

In 2004, calling Michael's sentence "cruel and unusual punishment" for such a miniscule amount of cocaine, he ordered Michael freed. Somehow the judge had found a loophole in the supposedly ironclad Three Strikes Law.

Later, after asking Michael to meet with him in his chambers, Letts ended up becoming the now former convict's mentor. When Michael stumbled and fell back into his old ways, the judge left his bench, went looking for him on Skid Row, eventually found him in the streets . . . and called the police. But instead of landing back in prison for yet another infraction, Michael found himself sentenced to the Dream Center.

Rather than lecturing his troubled friend, Judge Letts simply told him, "Michael, you've got a glorious chance here."[3]

During the past year Michael has found himself doing things he'd never imagined doing: picking up trash with a crew in Echo Park, handing out Christmas presents to impoverished kids, and even helping to build homes for the homeless.

More importantly, Michael has found a living faith in Jesus Christ that has given him the power and the motivation to walk a new path in life. He has discovered the truth of Philippians 2:13: "For it is God who is at work within you, *giving you the will and the power to achieve his purpose*" (PHILLIPS, italics mine).

A few months prior to this writing, Michael sent the *Times* reporter a letter. Here is a brief excerpt: "The Judge and Nancy [Webb, Judge Letts's assistant] have done the greatest thing they have ever done for me to date. They did not give up or allow me to give in. . . . I have been looking forward to the day I could tell you that I am doing well, and today I am doing very well. . . . Kurt, I don't understand how helping others turned out to be such a great help for me, and has changed me deep down within. . . . It's like a miracle."[4]

To me, even now as I watch these two friends out in the parking lot talking with such animation about God's goodness, I am struck by their incomparable story of one person believing in someone who couldn't even believe in himself. Theirs is a story of someone refusing to give up on a man who had already given up on himself.

Michael recently earned his GED and received a special acknowledgment of his achievement from the White House. Michael's story reminds me that God refuses to give up on the men and women He longs to redeem.

———

From time to time God seems to pull back the curtain just a little to give someone a glimpse of His will, His plan, His dream for his or her life.

For Cassandra Demman, that glimpse came in a rather unusual way and much earlier than she might have expected.

As a teenager who had chosen to walk on the wild side, Cassie began smoking pot and drinking by the time she was fifteen. Getting high helped her forget her many insecurities as well as the guilt she felt for some sexual encounters as a young child and for walking away from her parents' Christian faith.

As a result of her partying, Cassie began to pile up

underage drinking convictions. Most often the offense landed her in community service. Again and again, though, she ended up in one or the other of the same two places: serving meals at the local senior center or helping take meals to the elderly with Meals on Wheels.

And Cassie learned a funny thing about herself: she loved serving people. She enjoyed the very community service that had been intended as a punishment. The interaction reminded her of the times when she, as a young girl, helped her grandmother feed hungry children in their neighborhood. When one of those children grew up and opened up a food bank, the benefit came back to Cassie's own family, helping them through a time of need. That story had become part of family lore—it had been told and retold throughout her life.

So had God given Cassie a glimpse of His dream for her future? Something to give her hope and get her through the rebellious years when she walked a dark path far away from His will and intentions for her life?

Cassie was raised in a family of ten in the small town of Ironwood, Michigan, near the Canadian border. Her parents were Christians, and they tried to raise their children to follow the Lord. Cassie, however, chose the way of the world and her life steadily went downhill. Her behavior weighed on her heart and filled her with a fear of God's anger and punishment. Too frightened and ashamed to tell anyone what she had done, she held the secret in her heart—and the guilt and fear it caused weighed on her like a heavy stone,

"After I graduated from high school, I got a full-time job with a printing company. I figured that college just wasn't an option for me. Then I got into a relationship that became controlling and abusive. I felt powerless to change that situation, mostly because of my substance abuse problems. I would try to help my boyfriend, but I couldn't even help myself. After eight years of physical and emotional abuse—one time I was even pushed out of a moving car—I left that relationship and tried to move on with my life.

"I tried to go back to church, but I would end up drinking as soon as I walked out the doors. I just couldn't keep myself sober, so I thought I'd better hold off on God until I got myself cleaned up—if I ever could."

Taking a job as a bartender, Cassie drank herself into multiple blackouts. When she woke up, the pain from her hangovers was so intense that she eventually found herself hooked on painkillers. Then came the DUI, followed by a second. In time, the penalty was reduced to driving without a license.

As the binges and blackouts continued, Cassie saw her very life fragment and fall into so many broken, jagged shards that she despaired of piecing it back together again.

That's when she got the surprise call from her older sister, Rachel, who lived in Burbank. Rachel asked Cassie to come help her during a difficult pregnancy.

"I was surprised that I said yes," Cassie recalls. "If I were really able to help Rachel, it would be the first time I'd been sober in ten years.

"What had my life become? How had it happened? And what in the world could I do about it?"

Rachel, a Christian, took Cassie to a Saturday night

youth service at Angelus Temple and introduced her to a young woman in the discipleship program at the center.

"You ought to consider the program," Rachel told her troubled younger sister. "I know it would do you good."

Cassie declined. Entering the program would mean confronting her lifestyle and looking honestly at what she had become—and that thought was simply too overwhelming. So Cassie went back to Michigan and back to her old lifestyle of alcohol, pills, blackouts . . . and shame.

Rachel, however, didn't give up on her younger sister. She mailed Cassie an application for the Dream Center discipleship program.

"I wanted to fill it out," Cassie remembers, "but I would start to cry every time I tried. I knew I needed help, and deep down I knew that God was the only One who could fix me."

Cassie went back to Los Angeles to visit Rachel, who had already convinced Cassie to drop off an application.

During the short drive from the church to the center, though, Rachel got lost. The tour of the facilities they'd wanted to take had already started. Deeply discouraged, Cassie wondered if she had also lost the last opportunity to finally change her life. If they turned around now, would she ever have the courage to go back again?

The tour group, however, was just emerging from a building as Rachel and Cassie drove up. Somehow Pastor Murray, the designated tour guide that day, knew exactly why Cassie had come. Without her saying a thing to him, he knew she wanted to be in the tour and that she was interested in the program. Smiling kindly, he invited her to come along.

In that moment, Cassie felt enveloped with a peace beyond anything she had experienced in her entire life. "I knew this was going to be my home."

Yes, Cassie felt peace, but she soon found herself stretched like never before.

"God has constantly challenged me to believe in who He says I am." In her first year, for instance, Cassie had some opportunities to step into leadership roles—for the first time ever in her life.

But she couldn't process that: *Why are they trusting me? Why are they believing in me, believing that I can do things I've never done before?* The first time Cassie was put in charge of a cleaning crew, however, she had a panic attack and began weeping. Gently, her leaders helped her to trust in the Lord and push through her fear. And Cassie did.

"When Pastor Matthew started calling on me during tours to share my testimony, I would be sick to my stomach all day," Cassie remembers.

During those days of being stretched, however, Cassie heard the Lord Himself whisper words of comfort to her. He also gave her Isaiah 54:4 to hang on to in her fear: "Do not be afraid; you will not be put to shame. Do not fear disgrace; you will not be humiliated. You will forget the shame of your youth and remember no more the reproach of your widowhood" (NIV).

During her second year at the Dream Center, Cassie was asked not only to lead the women in their first year but also to teach a class, compelling her to confront her old fear of public speaking. Frightened as she may have been, Cassie held the Lord's hand and pushed on through it. Later she told her friends, "God always gives me grace."

Toward the end of that year, however, Cassie stumbled.

She had been invited to a wedding in Las Vegas, and when the guests began drinking in moderation, Cassie drank too. But for someone addicted to alcohol, moderation wasn't even an option.

Following that drinking bout, all of her old guilt and shame came flooding back and engulfed her: *Should I confess to my leaders what happened or keep it to myself? Should I quit the program? Should I give up on this new life as a lost and hopeless cause? Would the Lord give up on me?*

As Cassie wrestled with these questions, God once again spoke to her through His Word. In 1 Timothy 1:19, she read this: "Cling to your faith in Christ, and keep your conscience clear. For some people have deliberately violated their consciences; as a result, their faith has been shipwrecked" (NLT).

So Cassie confessed her lapse to her leaders and

accepted the discipline that followed. But rather than feeling shame or depression, a different and totally unexpected emotion seemed to blossom in her heart.

It was joy.

Yes, Cassie had stumbled. But God had walked her through it. The words of David were true: "The LORD directs the steps of the godly. He delights in every detail of their lives. Though they stumble, they will never fall, for the LORD holds them by the hand" (Psalm 37:23–24 NLT).

One day I said to her, "Cassie, I've been thinking and praying about it, and I really believe you are the one to take over our food truck ministry."

She looked at me with an expression that was a combination of shock and wonder. She knew that our food truck program is one of the largest and most important ministries we have.

"Why are you asking *me* to do this?" she said. "That's one of the biggest programs we have here. *Why are you believing in me?*"

Cassie confessed
her lapse to her
leaders and accepted
the discipline that
followed. But rather
than feeling shame
or depression, a
different and totally
unexpected emotion
seemed to blossom
in her heart.
It was joy.

"I believe in you," I told her, "because you have an undying love for the Lord. When you have that kind of passion for God, I know that He will help you work through anything and overcome any limitation."

Cassie then met with my wife, Caroline, who confirmed the choice: Cassie would become the director of one of our signature ministries.

"What an unbelievable honor," Cassie says on reflection. "This was the ministry that Pastor Caroline herself started years ago. I couldn't believe that she would place that kind of faith in me."

The first few weeks weren't easy, and once again Cassie had to confront her fears and bouts of panic. By this time, however, she and the Lord had walked through several new challenges together, and she had learned to push right through her fear and doubts whenever they arose.

And Cassie has excelled in this position. Under her wise and creative leadership, our feeding ministry is functioning at its highest level since its founding.

Because people believed in the hidden potential of the Lord's work in Cassie's life, she has been able to pass on that message of grace to people out at the food truck sites. That potential was always there, our staff just needed to show her the miracle that she is.

Cassie has led the food truck ministry for over two years now, is happily married to her "best friend," Matthew Demman, and has enrolled at the Angelus Bible Institute for further training, "so that I can be a better leader and teacher here at the Dream Center."

———

If you ever get a chance to visit us here in LA, you'll see happy, competent men and women serving meals, driving food trucks, teaching classes, and directing huge, important ministries that touch thousands of lives. With their backgrounds, some of these men and women wouldn't have a shot at many of the job opportunities and positions of responsibility in our city or nation. But the church of Jesus Christ uses more people who have been rejected by society than any other organization in the world does.

After all, we who follow Jesus love others because He

first loved us. We show grace because He has shown us grace. We believe in people who have stumbled and gotten to their feet again because time after time after time Jesus continues to believe in us after we stumble.

When God touches our heart, He allows us to believe in people we normally wouldn't believe in, to give hope to people who have all but given up on themselves, and to give second chances to people who would never expect a second chance.

Of course the choice still rests with every individual. Many parents might say, "I have believed in my child through some very dark times, but he still won't change" or "she still won't get moving in a positive direction."

Even so, the chances of people finally making a pivot in life and changing directions is exponentially stronger when they have a solid foundation of loving people supporting them—people who have spoken encouraging words to them and held out hope for their future.

Yes, they may wander away. But when God touches their heart, they have something to come back to. The odds of succeeding go up dramatically when you have someone who loves you and has expressed belief in you.

We believe in people who have stumbled and gotten to their feet again because time after time after time Jesus continues to believe in us after we stumble.

In Cassie, Caroline and I saw something that she didn't see in herself. We also believed in the work the Lord Himself was doing in her life. So even when she couldn't see hope or potential in her own future, she could draw on the hope we had in her potential and her future.

I also saw something else. Deep down, Cassie had a vision of helping people. It was a vision the Lord had given her when she was a little girl helping her grandmother feed hungry children in her neighborhood This vision grew stronger as she worked off public service sentences and served with Meals on Wheels.

The Lord Himself had long before given Cassie a glimpse of a possible future, and in spite of everything, she wanted to follow that vision.

She would never be satisfied with less.

Has the Lord given you a glimpse of His dream for your life?

Maybe, like Cassie, He gave you a glimpse when you

were just a child. Maybe it was when you were helping someone in a specific way, or maybe you were up to your ears in some activity and the Lord seemed to whisper, "You were made for this."

It doesn't matter how many years ago that moment may have occurred. It doesn't matter that you got off track rather than pursuing those dreams directly. And it doesn't matter if you're regretting all the time you feel like you've wasted. God is not only the One who gives you dreams but also the One who restores them.

And that restoration can begin today.

What Jesus Can Do for You

Has this ever happened to you?

You arrive at work, get out of the car, head to the elevator, walk into your office, and immediately get to your e-mail or pick up the phone. Preoccupied by that e-mail you need to send or that call you need to make, you sit down at your desk and realize you have only the vaguest sense of whom you passed by or greeted on the way in.

I sometimes have a similar vague sense about people I see when I arrive at the Dream Project, but for very different reasons. You see, when I get out of the car and walk across the parking lot, I will almost always see new people, but not all of those new people are recent arrivals. Yes, there are always a few individuals or families who have just arrived, whom I haven't met yet, who are just beginning a new chapter of life. But I'm talking about those men and women who have lived here for years, but who aren't anything at all like the people they were when they first walked through our doors. In that sense, they're new people.

By God's grace this place is filled with new people who have been through five, ten, even fifteen years of transformation. I'll bump into someone on campus and almost do a double take. I'll ask, "Did you graduate from here—maybe ten years ago?"

They will smile and say, "Yes, Pastor."

And I will shake my head and say, "You've been changed so much by Jesus that I hardly recognize who you are anymore."

That isn't just happy talk from the pastor; I mean it. I have seen changes so dramatic it would make you doubt your own eyes. Some of these people don't look at all like they did when they first arrived. Their countenances have changed. The way they walk has changed. Their voices have changed. Sometimes they're almost unrecognizable from the people they were when we first met.

That's the kind of transformation God can do for anyone. It's a reminder of how far He can take someone who fully surrenders to Him. I'm reminded of the New Testament story of Jesus' own transfiguration: the account tells us that "Jesus' appearance was transformed" (Matthew 17:2 NLT). His face was the one the disciples knew so well, yet . . . it wasn't. It was changed from the inside out. Peter, James, and John recognized Jesus, but in another sense they must have been saying, "Who is this Person? I don't even know who this is."

One woman I know won't *let* me forget who she once was.

On many of the tours I lead, this woman makes sure to remind me what God has done in her life—as if I could ever forget!

The first thing she does is whip out a picture of herself showing what she looked like when she first came through our doors. I've seen the picture dozens of times. Its edges have curled, and the color has begun to fade. And even though I've seen the photo, I always have to look again. In this woman's own words, she was a "strung-out junkie" addicted to crack cocaine. She weighed only about seventy-five pounds in those days, hardly more than a walking skeleton.

Then she waves the picture in my face and says, "Just look, Pastor. *Look!* Look at what Jesus has done for me!"

So I look again, and what I see always makes me smile. She's about seventy-five pounds heavier now, radiant with good health, professionally dressed, and overflowing with God's joy and passion. In the ten years she has been with us, she has become a nurse and now helps one of our doctors run our medical truck.

As I write these words, this woman is preparing for her wedding day in less than a week. We might even be losing her, but I have a feeling she'll find a way to keep putting that picture in front of my eyes. She'll probably have it scanned and e-mail it to me every day. She is excited about the work God has done in her life—and I love being reminded!

If you ever find yourself doubting the Lord's power to transform and redeem people's lives, if you ever start becoming a little blasé or cynical about the possibility that bruised and broken people can truly experience lasting change, take a little walk with me through the parking lot and wander through our buildings.

We could walk through the floor where our former prostitutes live. Many of them have come to the Lord and are now serving Him. You can see the shy smiles on their faces, because they've discovered that life can be fun again and even happy. They're daring to dream some big dreams again, and they're thinking about the future. And prostitutes keep coming. During a worship service, we'll have four or five come to the altar saying, "We've left the business because of what God can do."

On the first floor we'll meet up with a woman who always wants to show me her arms. "Pastor, look," she will say. "My arms are starting to heal from all the heroin needle marks." It's true: the old marks are fading in the same way that the shadows have faded from around her eyes. I'll give her a high five, and then we'll go up to the next floor to see the teen boys.

One of the eighteen-year-old boys, whose dad didn't want him, has been here since he was fifteen.

I'll often see him sitting beside his bed, reading his Bible.

"So what's your dream?" I will ask him.

He'll look up with a grin and say, "I want to be a pastor and take over your job someday."

I laugh and say, "Go ahead and do it!"

After I give him a big hug, we'll go on up to the next floor, where the homeless moms and dads are getting ready to go to work or take their kids to school.

As I linger on one of the floors or visit one of the houses on campus, I encounter more and more changed people. I see the faces of people who used to be addicts, drunks, prostitutes, counterfeiters, and car thieves, but who are now serving the Lord and making a difference in their community.

These people have not only changed, but they've *stayed* changed.

They're not only joyful, but they've been joyful for years.

They're not only rehabilitated, but they're giving everything they've got to rehabilitate others.

They've not only found hope after years of empty despair, but they've learned to give hope from the overflow in their own lives.

Finally, I'll get to my office on the eighth floor. But instead of sitting down in front of my computer, I will walk over to the windows and look out across the campus God has given us.

———

Back in 1926, the Franciscan Sisters of the Sacred Heart founded Queen of Angels Hospital on this site. At that time, Father Wilhelm Berger, founder of the order, defined their ministries as "works of neighborly love." With the establishment of the hospital, the sisters accepted the challenge to serve the poor, the sick, and the aging in Los Angeles, which they did for more than a half century.

I'm confident that, before a single shovelful of dirt was turned on the site, a great deal of prayer had gone into starting that hospital. I read somewhere that the nuns worked tirelessly to acquire the financial backing they needed to begin construction of the facility. The nuns even begged on the streets, and they were so devoted to the cause that they went hungry to save money for the endeavor. I don't know much about how Catholics do these things, but it's easy for me to imagine some faithful parishioners walking around the proposed site praying for the Lord's help and blessing.

So people had a vision for this place generations ago, many years before the Lord set my dad dreaming about a spiritual revival in urban Los Angeles.

Times change, neighborhoods change, demographics change, and cities change, but the Lord doesn't change, and I know the Lord hasn't forgotten any of those prayers. (Besides, God has a group of devoted Franciscan sisters up there in heaven to remind Him if He ever needs reminding.) And the Lord continues to respond to those prayers to this very day, although in a much different way than those devoted nuns and dear Catholic believers ever imagined.

Looking out over the campus from my windows, I'm overwhelmed with one thought: *Only Jesus could do this.* Only Jesus can take prostitutes, alcoholics, thieves, and emaciated drug addicts—only Jesus can take victims of abuse, neglect, abandonment, violence, and sometimes sheer satanic hatred—and transform them into hopeful, tenderhearted, clear-eyed men and women who are dreaming fresh dreams for their families and for their own life.

Urban experts, students, and social workers from all over the world visit our facilities to learn about our many programs. But no program in the world could accomplish what's being accomplished here. That's because the power is not in any program. The power for change is in Jesus.

The source of change is the supernatural love, compassion, forgiveness, and healing of God's Son, and I never, ever want to put any limits on what He can do.

That means that whatever impossible situation you are facing—health, marriage, finances, family—I'm here to tell you that I have seen impossibilities fall like dominoes before the power of Jesus Christ. We see it every day. You'd think I'd get used to it or become numb to it, but I never do.

Know that Jesus can bring back that son of yours who has been on drugs for twenty years. He can change the heart of your daughter, your wife, or your husband who has fallen further than you thought someone could fall. Jesus can give you a dream and the strength to follow it.

I know it sounds simplistic, but I have seen Jesus-powered change and transformation happen a thousand times in a thousand different ways over the last eighteen years.

One last story . . . just to encourage you that Jesus can change *anyone.*

My friend Barry Germain woke up one day under a freeway bridge, somewhere in Los Angeles, and asked himself, "What am I doing here?"

Barry had lived under that freeway bridge for fifteen years.

He was your classic homeless junkie, selling drugs, doing drugs, panhandling, trying to stay high, just barely making do. But life hadn't always been that way.

Barry was an educated man who had been a successful engineer. But when he lost his job, he went on a binge or two, and one thing led to another. In what seemed like an incredibly short period of time, he found himself living under a bridge. And that's where he stayed year after weary year for a big chunk of his life.

I had driven by Barry for years, and prayed for him. But year after year I saw no change in his life—or even an inclination to change. Then one day I was riding in my car with one of the teens from the Dream Center. When we saw Barry, she said very adamantly, "I've got to ask him to at least come to DC for a meal."

So she did. And Barry came. He showed up for dinner every night for six months, leaving just as soon as he was finished, returning to his place under the bridge. After half a year like this, I began to think Barry was taking advantage of the Dream Center. But God stopped me and said, "If you want to be a bridge of hope to the world, you've got to let yourself be walked on."

So we kept praying for Barry, and kept serving him dinner.

Then came the day when his life changed.

"If you want
to be a bridge
of hope to
the world,
you've got to
let yourself be
walked on."

"One day I was sitting under the bridge," Barry remembers, "just as I had for so many years. I found myself thinking that there had to be more to life than what I was doing. Like so many people do in desperate situations, I cried out to God."

It was the most desperate thing Barry Germain had ever done, and it changed everything. Why? Because God answered him immediately.

To his complete shock, Barry realized that there really was a God, that He had been listening, and that He had a dream for Barry's life.

This moment of salvation wasn't like a scene from a movie; it was even better. Barry's first experience with God was a small tidal wave of joy. "I can't explain it," he says, "but strangely enough—and all of a sudden—I began dancing and singing. That was my first encounter with really feeling God's presence. It wasn't until months later that I hopped on a Dream Center bus, because I knew I needed to change my life."

The Dream Center.

That's where I am investing my life. Here in inner city Los Angeles, where a great number of people have experienced really remarkable changes in their lives through the power of Jesus Christ. And that's the important point: you don't need a Dream Center; you just need to get hold of God's dream for you.

Barry goes on with his story:

"After fifteen years of living under a bridge, I began to dream again, to see hope in my life, and to see a future. After going through intense recovery and working through a lot of life-controlling issues that had landed me at rock bottom under that bridge, I was placed in charge of the food chapel here.

"Now, at sixty years old, I have completed Bible school. I'd had an education in my past life, but not a lot of smarts, or wisdom, if you know what I mean. But now God has rescued me, so I can help rescue others."

Now one of our pastors here in Los Angeles, Barry has a strong ministry to hundreds of homeless families.

God had a dream for Barry Germain, the most

unlikely candidate for a wise and compassionate pastor you will ever encounter.

The word *unlikely*, however, somehow never made it into God's dictionary. From one end of the Bible to the other, you read stories about the most improbable men and women whom He chose to be His prophets, disciples, ambassadors, representatives, and best friends.

And God has a dream for you, whoever you are, wherever you've been, and whatever you have or haven't accomplished during your years on earth.

That truth may be a little difficult to process. You might think, "I'm too young," or "I'm too old," or "I've missed my chance," or "I've made too many mistakes." Just remember that all of those so-called limitations aren't even blips on God's radar. They might seem big to you, but they are *nothing* to Him.

———

We've arrived at the end of this book, and I only have a little more space to convince you that at this moment . . .

right now . . . you are very, very close to grasping God's incomparable dream for your life.

The door is opening. Do you see it? *Walk through it.*

Jesus is reaching out to take your hand. *Take His.*

The minute you do that, I promise you, EVERYTHING changes.

God has a
dream for you,
whoever you
are, wherever
you've been, and
whatever you
have or haven't
accomplished
during your
years on earth.

Endnotes

1. Fernand Brunschwig, "Energy of a Slingshot: David & Goliath," accessed January 18, 2013, Wolfram Demonstrations Project; http://demonstrations.wolfram .com/EnergyOfASlingshotDavidAndGoliath/.
2. C. S. Lewis Pte. Ltd. 1946, *The Great Divorce* (San Francisco: Harper One, 2009), 77.
3. Kurt Streeter, "Justice and friendship prevail," *Los Angeles Times,* February 28, 2010, accessed January 18, 2013, http://articles.latimes.com/print/2010/feb/28/local/ la-me-judge-friendship28-2010feb28 and Kurt Streeter, "Despite stumbles an addict keeps a valued friend," Los Angeles Times, June 3, 2012, accessed January 18, 2013, http://articles.latimes.com/2012/jun/03/local/ la-me-streeter-20120604.
4. Ibid.

DREAMCENTER

the church that never sleeps

The Dream Center, a volunteer driven organization that finds and fills the needs of individuals and families alike, was founded in 1994 and currently serves over 50,000 people each month.

2301 Bellevue Avenue | Los Angeles CA 90026 | 213.273.7000

DREAMCENTER.ORG